Codependency: From Boundaries to Recovery

Breaking Free from the Interdependent Relationships Emotionally Trapping You from Your Next Steps Forward

Erica May

© Copyright 2024 - All rights reserved.

Legal Notice

used for personal use. Furthermore, it should not be shared with any other individual or persons for any purpose other than that for which it was initially intended. It is strictly prohibited to amend, reproduce, distribute, utilize, quote, or paraphrase any part of the content within this publication without prior authorization from the writer or publisher. Any violation of these regulations may result in legal action against those who have breached them.

Disclaimer Notice

The presented work is strictly informational and should not be interpreted as an offer to buy or sell any form of security, instrument, or investment vehicle. Furthermore, the information contained herein should not be taken as a medical, legal, tax, accounting, or investment recommendation given by the author(s) or any affiliated company, employees, or paid contributors. In other words, the information is presented without considering individual preferences for specific investments in terms of risk parameters. It is general information that does not account for a person's lifestyle and financial objectives. It is important to note that no tailored advice will be provided based on the given information.

Table of Contents

CHAPTER 4: BOUNDARIES: YOUR NEW BEST FRIENDS 51

CHAPTER 5: THE POWER OF NO: SETTING THE

CHAPTER 8: SEEKING SUPPORT: THERAPY AND BEYOND 93

CHAPTER 9: THE COMPANY YOU KEEP: HARNESSING THE POWER OF SUPPORT GROUPS 104

Welcome to the

Ideas Worth Sharing

Series

My name is Nicholas Bright, and I've spent nearly two decades working as a psychologist specializing in Behavioral Neuroscience and Interpersonal Communication in the US, UK, and Australia. Throughout my career, I've encountered countless stories, experiences, and insights that have shaped my understanding of the human mind and interpersonal interactions.

This series is a collaborative effort, bringing together the experience and expertise of myself and my colleagues: Erica May, Jeff Sharpe, Camila Alvarez, and potentially new faces in the future! We've chosen to write under pen names to respect everyone's privacy and keep the spotlight on the valuable content we offer rather than us as individuals. This decision allows us to freely share our knowledge without the distractions that often come with the limelight. We stand by the authenticity and credibility of the content shared here—our professional integrity remains at the forefront of this series.

We are deeply passionate about our field, and our primary goal is to equip you with practical, research-backed insights that you can implement in your everyday life. Each chapter is designed to inspire and help you better understand yourself and those around you.

We invite you to engage actively with the material: take notes, discuss the ideas with friends and family, and, most importantly, apply the lessons in your daily routine.

1. **Read;** understand what can be done to improve
2. **Reflect;** appreciate your feelings and their origins
3. **Remember;** put your learning into action

Thank you for embarking on this journey of knowledge and growth with us,

Nick

Want to Win Free Books?

Join Our Newsletter!

In this series, we appreciate that someone may find many different books helpful. I certainly know that when discussing sensitive topics like, for example, divorce, we can end up working on grief, anxiety, self-confidence, cognitive dissonance, and lots more. When we encounter a major challenge in life, it is rarely due to one small problem but rather a concoction of our experiences, outlooks, and actions; it's often a deep-rooted issue with many different things we need to uncover and support. We are complicated beings, and we must recognize this. As such, I would love to invite you all to join our newsletter.

In this, I aim to write articles of interest, including excerpts from various books in the series, as well as **vouchers**, **discounts**, and **giveaways**—and of course, no gimmicks or catches. I harbor a deep loathing of companies that offer seemingly amazing deals, only to charge you vast amounts in hidden fees! I vowed to never fall into that trap myself, and any offers I make are designed to be of true benefit and help. If you win a book in a giveaway, I want you to read it with a smile.

Join our newsletter and discover the additional value we can add to your life's curriculum!

Join us at: **www.IdeasWorthSharingSeries.com/newsletter**

See you on the inside!

About the Author: Dr. Erica May

Dr Erica May is a dedicated Clinical Psychologist practising in New York City. She graduated from Syracuse University in New York State, earning her degree in Clinical Psychology. Erica specializes in Cognitive Behavioral Therapy (CBT), Dialectical Behavior Therapy (DBT), and trauma-focused treatments. Her work is deeply rooted in helping individuals navigate complex emotional landscapes, enabling them to lead healthier and more fulfilling lives. Her compassionate approach and expertise have garnered her a reputation as a trusted mental health professional in her local community.

Erica has been friends and has worked with Nicholas Bright, the lead author of the Ideas Worth Sharing series, for many years. Together, they aim to help support a wider community by writing a book series on important topics within Psychology and extending their therapeutic insights and techniques beyond the confines of their practice. This book series will cover various topics related to mental health, including detailed guides on implementing CBT and DBT strategies in daily life, as well as comprehensive approaches to prevention, understanding and healing. By presenting practical exercises and learning through her practice, Erica hopes to make evidence-based psychological concepts more accessible to a broader audience. She aims to empower individuals with the knowledge and tools to manage their mental health proactively and independently, fostering greater resilience and well-being.

Preface

"Freedom is not the absence of commitments, but

the ability to choose – and commit myself

to – what is best for me."

Paulo Coelho

Embarking on the Journey to Self-Liberation: Unraveling Codependency and Cultivating Autonomy

At the heart of this book lies a journey towards self-liberation—a path that leads away from the suffocating grips of codependency and towards a life rich with autonomy and healthy relationships. The essence of this work is to unfold the often-misunderstood layers of codependency, providing you with a clear understanding of its manifestations and, more importantly, practical strategies for overcoming it.

I was compelled to write this book after witnessing numerous individuals struggle silently in relationships where their voices were barely a whisper against the needs of others. These people loved profoundly and gave unreservedly yet found themselves lost, their happiness tethered to the approval and presence of someone else. The stories ranged from a young woman who felt she couldn't pursue her career dreams because it might upset her partner to a devoted father who neglected his health while caring tirelessly for his family. Their journeys spoke of an urgent need for change—a call I felt deeply in my professional practice and personal encounters.

This book draws inspiration from various psychological theories and real-life success stories. It is enriched by contributions from mental health and wellness experts and my experiences as a counsellor helping individuals navigate their paths to emotional independence.

I extend my heartfelt gratitude to everyone who has supported this project—colleagues who provided insights, friends who encouraged persistence, and especially the brave souls who shared their personal stories, allowing us all to learn through their experiences.

By reading this book, you have taken a significant step towards embracing your true self and transforming your relationships. This is not just about learning; it's about changing. It's about not just surviving in your relationships but thriving within them.

The target audience for this work includes anyone who finds themselves repeatedly caught in cycles of codependent relationships—those who feel their well-being is overly dependent on the moods, actions, or approval of others. No prior knowledge is needed besides an open heart and a willingness to explore deep personal landscapes.

I thank you for your trust and commitment to this journey. As you turn each page, I invite you to engage actively with the strategies discussed and apply them in your life. Here's to finding freedom in choosing what's best for you—may you find profound empowerment and joy in the following pages.

Introduction

"Freedom lies in being bold."

Robert Frost

In personal growth and healthy relationships, the quest for autonomy and self-liberation is pivotal in many people's lives. It is a story that unfolds within the heart and mind, often hidden from the naked eye but deeply felt in the soul. This narrative is not for the faint-hearted; it demands courage, relentless introspection, and a commitment to change that can only come from within.

The essence of this exploration goes beyond simply diagnosing the ailment of codependency. It seeks to unearth the roots that bind individuals to patterns and behaviors that stifle growth and undermine personal and relational health. This journey invites readers to venture deep into the caverns of their psyche, challenging them to confront uncomfortable truths and reclaim the steering wheel of their lives.

The central thesis of our discussion situates the individual at a crossroads between past conditioning and the potential for future emancipation. It acknowledges that the legacy of codependency is not merely a personal struggle but a reflection of broader societal and relational dynamics. Through this lens, the path to liberation is both a deeply personal endeavor and a collective challenge, urging a paradigm shift in how relationships are perceived and navigated.

Empowerment emerges as a guiding theme throughout this narrative. Readers are not just passive recipients of information but active participants in their healing process. The text offers insights, analysis, practical tools, and exercises to foster self-awareness, resilience, and transformation. It is a handbook for those who no longer wish to be spectators in their lives but aspire to be the architects of their destiny.

Another vital aspect of this exploration is the redefinition of independence. Often misconstrued as isolation or emotional detachment, true freedom is portrayed as an interdependence that balances self-sufficiency with healthy, mutually enriching connections. This nuanced understanding underscores the importance of boundaries, not as barriers but as bridges towards more authentic and fulfilling relationships.

Mindfulness and self-compassion are core practices facilitating the transition from codependency to autonomy. Far from mere buzzwords, they are depicted as essential skills that enable individuals to stay grounded in their values and responsive to their needs. By cultivating mindful awareness of their thoughts, emotions, and behaviors, readers learn to navigate their inner world with compassion and clarity, setting the stage for genuine self-discovery and growth.

Reflecting on the narrative's progress, it becomes evident that the transformational arc from codependency to autonomy is both a conclusion and a commencement. It marks the end of old patterns that no longer serve and the beginning of a new chapter characterized by self-empowerment and intentional living. This dual nature of the journey underscores the cyclical process of growth, where every ending is a doorway to new possibilities.

The role of gratitude and self-forgiveness is underscored, highlighting their significance in the healing process. These practices are shown to catalyze change not just by modifying external behaviors but by transforming the inner landscape of beliefs and self-perceptions. Gratitude for the journey thus far and forgiveness for past missteps become pillars upon which a new sense of self is built.

This narrative invites readers to step into their power and claim a life marked by emotional balance and personal fulfillment. It presents a roadmap out of the shadows of codependency into the light of self-awareness, autonomy, and a renewed sense of connection with oneself and others. It is a testament to the resilience of the human spirit and the transformative power of self-realization.

Chapter 1: Unshackling the Mind: Understanding Codependency

"The best way to find yourself is to lose

yourself in the service of others."

Mahatma Gandhi

Are You Living Your Life, or Living for Others?

Understanding codependency is more than just a psychological exploration; it's about unlocking the chains that bind us to patterns of behavior that serve others at the expense of our well-being. This journey begins by confronting what codependency really is and how it has historically shaped relationships. Historically, codependency was identified in the context of relationships involving substance abuse, where one person enabled another's addiction. However, this concept has evolved to encompass a broader spectrum of behaviors where self-esteem and actions are excessively tied to pleasing others.

Defining codependency involves recognizing it as a pattern of sacrificing one's needs and blurring boundaries to maintain relationships, often leading to emotional and sometimes physical distress. Acknowledging these behaviours' surface interactions and deeper psychological and emotional roots is vital. These roots are usually planted early in life, stemming from family dynamics, societal expectations, or personal trauma. Understanding these origins is crucial for anyone looking to break free from these cycles.

Recognizing the signs of codependency can be transformative. Common indicators include a chronic need for approval, difficulty making decisions without reassurance from others, poor boundaries, and an obsessive preoccupation with the needs of others at the expense of one's own. Identifying these signs in oneself or relationship dynamics is the first step towards healing.

As we delve deeper into these patterns, we uncover the mechanisms through which individuals lose their sense of self. The recovery process is not about blame but understanding and gently dismantling these ingrained behaviors. This chapter serves as a foundation for the transformative advice detailed later in this book, focusing on fostering independence and building healthy, fulfilling relationships.

To reclaim your autonomy and begin the journey towards healthier relational dynamics, it is essential to establish clear personal boundaries. This helps define one's own space and limits and aids in mutual respect and understanding in relationships. Moreover, prioritizing self-care and validating one's emotions and needs are pivotal.

The overarching themes of this book revolve around empowerment through knowledge and action. By equipping yourself with an understanding of codependency and actively engaging with strategies to overcome it, you can transform your relationships within months—not just romantically but across all areas of your life, including friendships and professional connections.

In embracing these insights and strategies, readers will embark on a path not just toward recovery but toward a liberated life where the needs of others no longer shadow personal fulfillment. Each step forward in this book builds upon foundational knowledge towards realizing a balanced existence free from the constraints of past dependencies.

Codependency is a complex and often misunderstood phenomenon that can profoundly impact relationships and personal well-being. At its core, codependency involves an excessive reliance on others for validation, approval, and a sense of identity. This pattern of behavior can lead to a lack of boundaries, difficulty in asserting one's needs, and a constant prioritization of others' feelings and desires over one's own. Understanding codependency involves recognizing the detrimental effects it can have on one's mental health and relationships.

Historically, the term "codependency" originated in the context of addiction treatment. It described the enabling behavior of family members or partners of individuals struggling with substance abuse. Over time, the concept expanded to encompass a broader range of unhealthy relationship dynamics beyond addiction. Today, codependency is recognized as a pattern of behavior characterized by emotional dependence, low self-esteem, and an intense fear of abandonment.

Codependent individuals often struggle with setting boundaries, expressing their needs openly, and prioritizing self-care. They may feel responsible for others' emotions and well-being to an unhealthy degree, leading to feelings of resentment, anxiety, and emotional exhaustion. Recognizing these patterns within oneself is the first step towards breaking free from codependency.

By understanding the historical context of codependency and its impact on personal relationships, individuals can unravel the complex web of behaviors contributing to this dynamic. Empowering oneself with knowledge about codependency can pave the way for transformative growth and healthier relationship patterns.

Unraveling the Psychological Roots of Codependency: Understanding and Breaking Free

Codependent behaviors often have deep-seated psychological and emotional roots that can be traced back to early life experiences and learned patterns of relating to others. Understanding these roots is crucial in unraveling the complexities of codependency. Many individuals who exhibit codependent tendencies have grown up in environments where their emotional needs were not adequately met, leading them to seek validation and approval from external sources to fill the void within themselves.

Childhood experiences of neglect, abuse, or inconsistent caregiving can shape the development of codependent behaviors. Growing up in a household where boundaries were blurred and roles were unclear can foster a sense of insecurity and a need for control in relationships. Individuals may have learned to prioritize others' needs over their own, equating love with self-sacrifice and caretaking.

Low self-esteem and a lack of self-worth are common threads woven into the fabric of codependency. Feelings of unworthiness or inadequacy can drive individuals to seek validation externally, relying on others to affirm their values and identity. This perpetual cycle of seeking validation from others perpetuates codependent patterns and reinforces a sense of dependency on external sources for self-worth.

Fear of abandonment or rejection often underlies codependent behaviors. Individuals may go to great lengths to avoid conflict or disapproval, sacrificing their own needs and desires to maintain harmony in relationships. This fear can lead to an excessive focus on pleasing others, even at the expense of one's well-being.

Unresolved trauma and unmet emotional needs from the past can manifest as codependency in adulthood. The wounds of the past may resurface in current relationships, driving individuals to seek healing through unhealthy dynamics that mirror past experiences. Without addressing these underlying emotional wounds, breaking free from codependent patterns can be challenging.

Codependency is not simply a behavior; it is often a coping mechanism developed in response to adverse circumstances. By recognizing the psychological and emotional roots of codependency, individuals can begin the journey towards healing and self-discovery. Acknowledging these roots is the first step towards breaking free from codependent patterns and reclaiming autonomy.

Identifying these psychological and emotional roots is essential in unraveling the complexities of codependency and paving the way for meaningful change. By delving into these underlying factors with compassion and self-reflection, individuals can begin to untangle the web of codependency that has held them captive. Through introspection, therapy, and self-compassion, individuals can gradually release themselves from codependency and embark on a path towards self-empowerment and healthier relationships.

Recognizing the signs of codependency in oneself and

relationships is a crucial step towards breaking free from unhealthy patterns and reclaiming autonomy. It involves introspection, honesty, and a willingness to confront uncomfortable truths. Self-awareness is the key to unlocking the chains of codependency and fostering healthier relationships with oneself and others.

One common sign of codependency is an excessive need for approval and validation from others. This constant seeking of external validation can stem from deep-seated insecurities and a lack of self-worth. Individuals may find themselves constantly seeking reassurance from their partners or loved ones, basing their self-esteem on the opinions of others rather than their sense of self.

Another sign is difficulty setting boundaries. Codependent individuals often have porous borders, allowing others to dictate their thoughts, feelings, and actions. This lack of personal boundaries can lead to resentment, being taken advantage of, and losing individual identity within relationships.

People-pleasing tendencies are also indicative of codependency. Constantly putting others' needs before one's own, even at the expense of personal well-being, can be a sign of underlying codependent behaviors. The fear of rejection or abandonment drives this compulsion to prioritize others over oneself.

Avoidance of conflict is another red flag. Codependent individuals may go to great lengths to avoid conflict or confrontation in their relationships, sacrificing their own needs and desires to maintain harmony at all costs. This avoidance often stems from a fear of rejection or abandonment if they assert themselves.

A distorted sense of responsibility for others' emotions and actions is also prevalent in codependency. Taking on the role of caretaker or savior in relationships can lead to emotional exhaustion and neglecting one's needs.

Recognizing these signs in oneself requires honesty and introspection. It involves acknowledging the patterns that have kept you trapped in unhealthy dynamics and taking steps towards breaking free from them. By identifying these behaviors, you can cultivate healthier relationship patterns based on mutual respect, communication, and boundaries.

Facing these signs head-on is empowering. It allows you to reclaim your sense of self, establish healthy boundaries, and prioritize your well-being above seeking validation from others. Remember that recognizing these signs is not a sign of weakness but a courageous step towards liberation from codependency's chains.

Having explored the multifaceted nature of codependency, from its historical underpinnings to its psychological roots and outward signs, we stand at a crucial juncture. The journey ahead promises not just insight but transformative action that can radically alter the course of your personal and relational well-being.

Recognizing codependent behaviors is just the beginning. The true challenge—and opportunity—lies in confronting and reshaping these patterns. This process isn't merely about adjustment; it's about reclamation of your autonomy and fostering a profound sense of self-empowerment. By setting healthy boundaries and prioritizing your emotional needs, you engage in an act of profound self-respect.

As you progress through this book, each chapter builds on the last, equipping you with practical tools and strategies that are both easy to implement and profoundly influential. These tools are designed to help you step back from seeking external validation and cultivate a robust internal support system instead.

Embrace this journey with an open heart and a willing mind. The path to overcoming codependency is rich with challenges but even more rewarding. You will discover strengths you never knew you had and develop skills to improve your relationships and enhance your quality of life.

Take control, engage actively with the techniques provided, and remember you can master your emotions and transform your life. The power to change lies within your grasp; use it to forge a future where your relationships are healthy, balanced, and mutually supportive.

Let's embark on this empowering journey together, embracing change with courage and optimism. The road to recovery is before you—confidently step forward and claim the fulfilling life you deserve.

Chapter 2: Childhood Echoes: The Genesis of Codependency

"I am not an island, entire of itself; every man

is a piece of the continent."

John Donne

Are You Repeating Your Childhood Without Realizing It?

When we think about the roots of codependency, it's common to consider only the surface behaviors—people pleasing, difficulty in setting boundaries, or a chronic need to care. However, these behaviors often stem from deeper psychological patterns ingrained during childhood. To break free from the chains of codependency, as explored in this chapter, we must first understand how our earliest experiences shape our current relational dynamics.

Childhood experiences play a pivotal role in shaping adult relationships, especially for those who find themselves repeatedly entangled in codependent patterns. These early years are not just about the overt neglect or abuse that some might face; they also encompass the subtle dynamics of caregiving and emotional availability—or lack thereof—that form the blueprint of our future selves. By unpacking these formative moments, individuals can gain critical insights into their relational behaviors and motivations.

Inconsistent caregiving is one such childhood experience that has profound implications for adult codependency. When caregivers oscillate between over-involvement and neglect, children learn to associate love with instability. This learned behavior can manifest in adulthood as a constant need to secure affection and approval from others, often at a high personal cost. Understanding this linkage is crucial for anyone seeking to overcome their codependent tendencies.

Emotional neglect, while less overt than physical neglect or abuse, can be equally damaging. It involves consistently disregarding the child's emotional needs, leaving them feeling fundamentally unseen or misunderstood. Adults who grew up in such environments may develop a heightened sensitivity to other's emotions as a survival tactic, inadvertently setting the stage for codependent relationships where their own needs are perpetually sidelined.

Reflection on personal history is not merely an academic exercise but a vital step towards healing. Recognizing early patterns of codependency involves asking oneself challenging questions about past relationships and interactions within one's family of origin. Were there moments when you felt your needs were consistently overlooked? Did you find yourself frequently stepping into caretaker roles even as a child? Answers to these questions can illuminate current relational patterns and provide a roadmap for change.

Encouraging readers to take control of their situations underscores that change is possible. This empowerment is crucial because understanding alone does not lead to change; action does. Implementing simple yet effective strategies like setting boundaries, practicing self-reflection, and seeking therapeutic support can transform knowledge into tangible improvements in relationships and self-esteem.

The journey toward breaking free from codependency begins with a compassionate inquiry into one's past, coupled with a commitment to applying this newfound knowledge actively in daily life. By addressing these childhood echoes head-on, individuals improve their lives and potentially break cycles of dysfunction for generations to come.

This exploration is both challenging and deeply rewarding—offering freedom from past constraints and a more straightforward path toward healthier, more autonomous futures. Remember: the strength for transformation lies within your grasp, and taking those first steps can lead you toward truly liberated living.

Understanding codependency involves delving into the roots of this complex pattern, particularly in childhood experiences. Childhood plays a pivotal role in shaping our behaviors and beliefs, often laying the foundation for how we interact with others in our adult lives. When it comes to codependency, early experiences of inconsistent caregiving or emotional neglect can significantly contribute to the development of codependent tendencies. These childhood echoes reverberate throughout our lives, influencing how we perceive ourselves, our worth, and our relationships.

Inconsistent caregiving can profoundly impact a child, fostering a sense of uncertainty and insecurity. When caregivers are unpredictable or unreliable in meeting a child's needs, the child learns to adapt by prioritizing others' needs over their own. This sets the stage for codependent behaviors, where individuals become hyper-focused on taking care of others while neglecting their well-being. The seeds of self-neglect are sown in these early experiences, leading to a pattern of seeking validation and approval from external sources.

Emotional neglect is another critical factor that can contribute to the development of codependency. When children's emotional needs are consistently unmet or dismissed, they learn to suppress and prioritize others' feelings instead. This ingrained pattern can manifest in adulthood as an overwhelming urge to please others at the expense of one's happiness and fulfillment. The cycle perpetuates as individuals seek external validation to fill the void left by emotional neglect.

Reflecting on these childhood experiences is essential in

unraveling the complexities of codependency. By examining the roots of these patterns, individuals can gain insight into why they engage in certain behaviors and how these behaviors impact their relationships. Self-awareness is critical to breaking free from codependent tendencies, as it allows individuals to recognize harmful patterns and make conscious choices to change them.

Exploring Childhood Roots: Unraveling Codependency for Healing and Transformation

By understanding the role of childhood experiences in fostering codependency, individuals can begin to unravel the intricate web of behaviors that have shaped their relationships. Empowering yourself with this knowledge opens the door to healing and transformation, paving the way for healthier, more fulfilling connections based on mutual respect and boundaries. Through introspection and self-discovery, it is possible to break free from the chains of codependency and embrace a liberated life filled with authenticity and self-love.

Understanding how inconsistent caregiving and emotional neglect contribute to codependent tendencies is crucial in unraveling the complexities of this behavior pattern. Inconsistent caregiving can manifest in various forms, such as unpredictable responses to a child's needs or intermittent displays of affection. These erratic patterns can leave a child uncertain about their worth and value, leading them to seek validation and approval externally, which can later translate into codependent behaviors in adulthood.

Emotional neglect, often overlooked but profoundly impactful, occurs when a child's emotional needs are consistently unmet or dismissed. This neglect can instill a deep sense of unworthiness and inadequacy, driving individuals towards seeking validation and acceptance from others to fill the emotional void left by childhood neglect. Codependency can thus emerge as a coping mechanism for the unmet emotional needs of the past.

Recognizing the role of inconsistent caregiving and emotional neglect in fostering codependency is the first step towards breaking free from these patterns. Acknowledging that these experiences have shaped your relational dynamics is empowering, as it allows you to reclaim agency over your behaviors and responses. By understanding the roots of codependency, you can begin to untangle the web of unhealthy relational patterns that have been ingrained since childhood.

Developing self-awareness is critical to addressing codependent tendencies rooted in inconsistent caregiving and emotional neglect. You can gain insights into your behavioural patterns and triggers by reflecting on past experiences and recognizing how they have influenced your current relationships. Self-reflection enables you to identify areas for growth and healing, paving the way for healthier interactions based on mutual respect and boundaries.

Seeking therapy or support groups specialized in codependency can provide valuable tools and strategies to navigate the complexities of these deeply ingrained patterns. Therapeutic interventions such as cognitive-behavioral therapy (CBT) or dialectical behavior therapy (DBT) can help reframe negative beliefs stemming from childhood experiences and cultivate healthier coping mechanisms.

Practicing self-care and setting boundaries is essential in breaking free from codependent tendencies rooted in inconsistent caregiving and emotional neglect. Prioritizing your well-being, nurturing yourself emotionally, and establishing clear boundaries in relationships are foundational steps towards reclaiming autonomy and fostering healthier connections based on reciprocity.

Understanding how inconsistent caregiving and emotional neglect contribute to codependent tendencies provides a roadmap for healing and transformation. By delving into the emotional roots of codependency, individuals can embark on a journey of self-discovery, self-compassion, and, ultimately, liberation from unhealthy relational dynamics.

Reflecting on your personal history is a crucial step in recognizing early patterns of codependency. By looking back at your childhood experiences and relationships, you can gain valuable insights into the roots of your codependent tendencies. Take a moment to explore how your caregivers interacted with you during your formative years. Were they consistent in their emotional support and availability, or did you experience neglect or inconsistency in their care?

Understanding how these early dynamics shaped your beliefs and behaviors can be eye-opening. It's common for codependency to stem from childhood experiences where emotional needs were not consistently met. This lack of emotional nurturing can lead to seeking validation and approval from others later in life, often at the expense of one's needs and well-being.

Take a compassionate approach when reflecting on these early patterns. Understand that these behaviors were likely coping mechanisms developed in response to challenging circumstances. Recognize that acknowledging these patterns is the first step towards healing and breaking free from codependency.

Identifying specific instances from your past where you felt the need to prioritize others' feelings over your own can be enlightening. These moments may reveal recurring themes or triggers that contribute to your codependent tendencies. By shining a light on these patterns, you empower yourself to make conscious choices moving forward.

Consider seeking support from a therapist or counselor to delve deeper into these childhood echoes and their impact on your current relationships. A professional can provide guidance and tools to help you navigate through past traumas and develop healthier coping mechanisms.

Practice self-compassion as you uncover these early patterns. Remember that it takes courage to confront past wounds and work towards healing. Embrace this journey of self-discovery with kindness and understanding towards yourself.

Journaling can be a powerful tool for reflecting on your personal history and identifying key moments that shaped your codependent tendencies. Write down any memories or emotions that arise during this process, allowing yourself to process and make sense of them at your own pace.

By recognizing early patterns of codependency, you pave the way for transformation. Embrace this opportunity for self-awareness and growth, knowing that by understanding the past, you can create a more empowered future free from the chains of codependency.

Understanding the roots of codependency is essential to overcoming its hold on our lives. This chapter has highlighted that codependency often originates from childhood experiences, mainly through inconsistent caregiving and emotional neglect. These early interactions shape our emotional landscape and set the stage for future relationships.

Recognizing these patterns is more than an exercise in self-awareness; it is a crucial step towards healing. By reflecting on your personal history, you can identify behaviors that may have been adaptive as a child but are maladaptive in adulthood. Awareness is the first step towards change, and this understanding empowers you to start making different choices.

The journey to overcoming codependency requires courage and commitment, but it is entirely achievable. Implementing small, consistent changes in how you relate to others and yourself can lead to significant transformations. Start by setting boundaries, practicing self-care, and seeking support when needed. Each step forward is a move towards a more autonomous and fulfilling life.

Embrace the challenge of change with the confidence that you are not alone in this journey. Many have walked this path before you, transforming their struggles into strengths. Let their successes inspire you as you embark on your path to liberation.

Remember, overcoming codependency is not about reaching a perfect state but about progressing towards healthier, more balanced relationships. With each step, you reclaim a piece of yourself and move closer to a life defined not by past dependencies but by present resilience and future possibilities.

Chapter 3: Breaking the Cycle: Confronting Codependent Behaviors

"The only real prison is fear, and the only real freedom is freedom from fear."

Aung San Suu Kyi

Are You Stuck in a Dance of Dependency?

Imagine waking up each day feeling empowered and independent, free from the exhausting tug-of-war of codependent relationships. This vision can become your reality as we delve into transformative strategies designed to break the cycle of codependency. The journey toward healing is not just about altering a few behaviors; it's a holistic transformation that integrates setting boundaries, understanding your inner child, and practicing self-compassion.

Acknowledging the need for change is the foundational step in this transformative process. It is crucial to recognize and accept that the patterns you are experiencing are not conducive to a healthy, fulfilling life. This self-awareness paves the way for profound healing and is often the most challenging step because it requires confronting uncomfortable truths about oneself and one's relationships.

Once acknowledgment is secured, the practical phase begins. Here, you will be introduced to exercises and worksheets tailored to help you identify specific codependent patterns in your behavior. These tools provide insight and foster an environment where you can practice new behaviors safely and constructively. By repeatedly engaging with these exercises, you solidify new habits that support your autonomy and personal growth.

The next pivotal step involves developing strategies to challenge and change existing relationship dynamics contributing to codependent behaviors. This might include learning to say no without feeling guilty, asking for what you need without fear, and recognizing when others are crossing your boundaries. Each strategy reinforces the notion that you deserve relationships marked by mutual respect and equality.

Healing from codependency also involves deep emotional work, mainly through inner child work and self-compassion practices. These techniques allow you to heal past wounds that often fuel codependent tendencies and help you develop a nurturing inner voice—a stark contrast to the critical or neglectful internal dialogues that frequently accompany codependency.

Building emotional resilience is another critical aspect of breaking free from codependent patterns. It involves developing the ability to cope with stressors and emotional upheavals without reverting to old habits. Emotional resilience empowers you to face life's challenges with confidence and stability, ensuring that setbacks do not derail your progress toward healthier relational dynamics.

By embracing these strategies, you take control of your emotional well-being and set the stage for healthier interpersonal relationships. Each step forward in this chapter is a step toward a more liberated life where your needs are met, your boundaries respected, and your personal growth celebrated. Remember, breaking free from codependency is not just about changing how you interact with others; it's about transforming how you see and treat yourself—a journey well worth embarking on.

Healing from codependency begins with acknowledging the need for change and recognizing the role of self-acknowledgment in the journey towards recovery. It is essential to understand that breaking free from codependent behaviors requires a conscious effort to unravel ingrained patterns and cultivate self-awareness. By acknowledging the need for change, you are taking the first step towards reclaiming your sense of self and establishing healthier relationships.

Self-acknowledgment plays a crucial role in healing from codependency, as it involves recognizing your own needs, emotions, and boundaries. This process allows you to differentiate between your feelings and those of others, fostering a deeper understanding of your identity. By acknowledging your worth and value, you can set boundaries that protect your emotional well-being and establish a sense of autonomy.

Self-acknowledgment is not about self-blame or criticism but rather about self-compassion and acceptance. It involves embracing your strengths and vulnerabilities allowing yourself to be imperfect and human. Accepting yourself fully paves the way for genuine growth and transformation.

Practicing self-acknowledgment involves being honest about your thoughts, feelings, and behaviors. It requires self-reflection and introspection, allowing you to explore the underlying reasons behind your codependent tendencies. By confronting uncomfortable truths with compassion, you can begin to unravel the complex web of codependency and work towards building healthier relationship dynamics.

Empowering Transformation: Practical Exercises for Breaking Free from Codependency

In breaking free from codependent patterns, practical exercises and worksheets are pivotal in identifying and unraveling these profoundly ingrained behaviors. Self-awareness is the first step towards transformation, and these tools provide a structured approach to recognizing codependency in one's life. Individuals can start dissecting their relationships, emotions, and reactions by engaging in these exercises to uncover the underlying dynamics.

Reflective worksheets can serve as mirrors, reflecting patterns that might have gone unnoticed. Through guided questions and prompts, individuals can begin to see recurring themes in their interactions with others. These exercises can help pinpoint moments where boundaries were crossed, self-worth was compromised, or needs were neglected in favor of others. This clarity is crucial in understanding the root causes of codependency.

Role-playing scenarios can also be a powerful tool to simulate real-life situations where codependent behaviors typically arise. Individuals can gain insights into their reactions and thought processes by stepping into different roles and perspectives. This exercise can shed light on automatic responses stemming from codependent tendencies, paving the way for conscious choices in similar situations.

Journaling prompts offer a safe space for introspection and emotional processing. Writing down thoughts, feelings, and experiences can provide a cathartic release while uncovering patterns contributing to codependency. Journaling regularly allows individuals to track their progress, setbacks, and moments of growth along their journey towards healthier relationships.

Visualization techniques can help individuals envision a life free from codependency. By imagining themselves setting boundaries confidently, asserting needs, and nurturing self-care practices, they begin to rewire their subconscious beliefs. Visualization reinforces the idea that change is possible and instils a sense of empowerment to take actionable steps towards breaking the cycle of codependency.

Accountability partners or support groups can enhance the effectiveness of these exercises by providing external validation and encouragement. Sharing insights, progress, and challenges with trusted individuals creates a sense of community and shared experience. Accountability partners can offer feedback, perspective, and gentle reminders when old patterns resurface, reinforcing the commitment to personal growth.

Incorporating these practical exercises into daily routines fosters a continuous process of self-discovery and transformation. Consistent engagement with these tools and a willingness to confront uncomfortable truths and emotions set the stage for lasting change. Each exercise serves as a building block towards dismantling codependent behaviors and establishing healthier relationship dynamics based on authenticity, respect, and mutual support.

By actively participating in these exercises with dedication and openness, individuals pave the way for profound shifts in their relational patterns. The journey towards liberation from codependency begins with small but intentional steps towards self-awareness and empowerment through actionable practices that lead to transformative outcomes in relationships and personal well-being.

Process Model: Codependency Breakthrough Framework

A Process Model is essential to challenge existing codependent behaviors effectively. This model guides individuals through a structured pathway from recognizing codependent patterns to actively breaking free from them. The model comprises three crucial components: self-awareness, acknowledgment, and initiation of change.

Self-Awareness

The first step in the framework involves enhancing self-awareness regarding codependent tendencies. This phase prompts individuals to reflect on their fears, expectations, and how they seek validation from others. Individuals gain insights into their behavior patterns and underlying motivations by asking reflective questions and delving into these aspects.

Acknowledgment

After fostering self-awareness, the next stage is acknowledgment. This component emphasizes accepting one's codependent traits without judgment. It is the cornerstone for transformation, allowing individuals to recognize their behaviors without shame or guilt. Embracing these traits with compassion opens the door to meaningful change.

Initiation of Change

The final phase of the model focuses on initiating tangible change. It presents practical exercises and challenges aimed at gradually dismantling codependent behaviors. Techniques such as journaling instances of codependency, setting achievable independence goals, and reducing dependency on external validation are introduced. These steps prioritize incremental progress and emphasize patience in breaking free from codependency.

By intertwining self-awareness, acknowledgment, and initiation of change, this framework offers a comprehensive approach to addressing codependent behaviors. Each component builds upon the other, creating a roadmap for individuals to navigate their path toward healthier relationships and increased self-reliance.

The dynamics of this model revolve around a continuous loop of self-discovery, acceptance, and growth. As individuals progress through each phase, they deepen their understanding of themselves, cultivate self-compassion, and gradually shift their behaviors towards independence and emotional resilience.

Practically, this framework equips individuals with actionable strategies to challenge existing relationship dynamics and break free from codependent patterns. By encouraging small steps towards change and emphasizing self-acceptance throughout the process, individuals can build a foundation for lasting transformation in their relationships.

In summary, the Codependency Breakthrough Framework provides a structured approach for individuals to confront and overcome codependent behaviors. This model empowers individuals to reclaim their autonomy and cultivate healthier relationships built on mutual respect and boundaries by fostering self-awareness, promoting acknowledgment without judgment, and initiating gradual change.

Embracing Change

The journey to overcoming codependency begins with the courage to acknowledge the need for change. Recognizing your patterns is the first step toward healing, and this acknowledgment is a powerful act of self-care. It sets the stage for a transformative process that benefits you and enhances your relationships.

Practical Tools for Self-Discovery

Implementing practical exercises and worksheets is a cornerstone in identifying and understanding your codependent behaviors. These tools offer clear insights into your relational dynamics, providing a structured way to reflect on your interactions and emotions. By engaging actively with these resources, you pave the way for meaningful change, fostering a more profound sense of self-awareness.

Strategies for Relationship Renewal

Developing strategies to challenge existing relationship dynamics is crucial. This involves setting healthy boundaries, engaging in honest communication, and prioritizing well-being. These strategies empower you to build relationships that are balanced and fulfilling. Remember, changing deeply ingrained behaviors takes time and persistence, but each step forward is a move towards a more liberated life.

Taking Action

The path to healing from codependency is not passive; it requires active engagement with both self and others. By applying the strategies discussed, you embrace your innate capacity for growth and resilience. This proactive approach heals and enriches your life, leading to genuinely supportive and freeing relationships.

Continuous Growth

Healing is an ongoing journey. Continue to apply these insights and techniques in your daily life. Each day, you'll find yourself more adept at navigating relationship complexities with increased confidence and clarity. Your efforts will cultivate an environment where personal fulfillment and mutual respect thrive.

By embracing these practices, you affirm your commitment to living a life defined not by dependency but by the richness of self-discovery and renewed connections. Embrace this journey with openness, knowing that each step forward shapes a future where your emotional health is the cornerstone of every relationship.

Chapter 4: Boundaries: Your New Best Friends

"Do not go where the path may lead, go instead where

there is no path and leave a trail."

Ralph Waldo Emerson

Discover the Power of Saying No: How Boundaries Can Transform Your Life

Establishing healthy boundaries can seem daunting in a world where relationships often define our self-worth and decision-making. However, the journey toward breaking free from codependency begins with understanding the critical role boundaries play in our lives. They are not just barriers but the foundation upon which mutual respect and genuine connection are built. For those entangled in codependent dynamics, recognizing and asserting one's needs is a vital step towards emotional liberation.

Boundaries are essential for anyone seeking to reclaim their autonomy and enhance their well-being. By defining what is acceptable and what isn't in our interactions, we protect our mental health and foster relationships that respect our individuality. This chapter delves into why setting these limits is crucial, particularly in overcoming codependency. It highlights how boundaries can prevent us from losing ourselves in the needs and desires of others, thereby promoting an environment where both parties can thrive authentically.

The process of establishing boundaries often starts with self-reflection. Understanding your own needs, values, and limits is paramount. For many, this self-discovery can be challenging, as codependency blurs the lines of individual preferences and desires. Once these personal standards are identified, the next step involves communicating them to others. This communication must be direct yet respectful, ensuring your message is understood but not aggressive.

Enforcing these boundaries is perhaps the most challenging part, especially for those accustomed to prioritizing others' needs above their own. It requires consistent effort; sometimes, you face uncomfortable situations and must stand firm in your decisions. This assertion of one's limits is not an act of selfishness but a profound form of self-respect.

Step-by-Step Guide to Setting Healthy Boundaries

Step 1: Reflect on Your Needs and Values

Take time to understand what truly matters to you. Reflect on past experiences where you felt compromised or drained—these moments can offer insights into where boundaries are needed.

Step 2: Identify Your Boundaries

List specific areas— your time, emotional energy, physical space, or other aspects—that need protection based on your reflections.

Step 3: Communicate Your Boundaries Clearly

Choose an appropriate moment to discuss your boundaries with those involved. Use "I" statements to keep the focus on your feelings and needs without blaming or accusing others.

Step 4: Enforce Your Boundaries

Stay firm and consistent. If someone crosses a boundary, remind them of your limits clearly and assertively.

Step 5: Practice Self-Care

Engage in activities that fortify your mental health and reaffirm your right to set boundaries. Self-care acts as both a reinforcement of boundaries and a reward for maintaining them.

Step 6: Reevaluate and Adjust Boundaries as Needed

As you grow and circumstances change, so too should your boundaries. Regularly assess their effectiveness and make adjustments as necessary.

This systematic approach helps set up effective boundaries that align with your evolving life context. Each step builds upon the previous one, creating a robust framework that supports personal growth and healthier relationships.

By embracing these practices, individuals struggling with codependency can begin to see significant improvements in their interactions and overall quality of life. The empowerment that comes from effectively setting boundaries is transformative— turning previous patterns of submissiveness into acts of strength and self-respect.

Setting and maintaining healthy boundaries is crucial for breaking free from the chains of codependency. Understanding the importance of boundaries is the foundational step towards transforming relationships into more nutritious, more balanced dynamics. Boundaries serve as the invisible lines that define where you end and others begin, protecting your sense of self-worth and autonomy. Without clear boundaries, codependent patterns can easily take root, leading to feelings of resentment, suffocation, and emotional exhaustion.

Boundaries are not selfish; they are self-care. They are essential for maintaining emotional well-being and fostering healthy relationships. By setting boundaries, you communicate your needs, values, and limits to others, allowing mutual respect and understanding to flourish. Boundaries empower you to prioritize your mental and emotional health while respecting the boundaries of those around you.

Establishing healthy boundaries creates a safe space for authentic communication and emotional balance within your relationships. Boundaries are not walls but bridges that connect individuals through honest and respectful interactions. They enable you to express your true self without fear of judgment or rejection, fostering genuine connections based on mutual trust and acceptance.

Without boundaries, it becomes challenging to distinguish where you end, and others begin, leading to enmeshed relationships where personal identities blur together. Healthy boundaries promote individuality within relationships, allowing each person to maintain their unique identity while being part of a collective partnership. This balance is essential for cultivating fulfilling connections built on authenticity rather than dependency.

Empowering Relationships: Setting and Communicating Boundaries with Confidence

Setting and communicating boundaries with family, friends, and partners is crucial for breaking free from codependent relationships. Effective communication of boundaries involves clarity, assertiveness, and consistency. When establishing boundaries, being direct and specific about what behaviors are acceptable and unacceptable to you is essential. Instead of assuming others will naturally understand your needs, clearly and respectfully articulate them.

Start by reflecting on your boundaries before communicating them to others. Understand what makes you uncomfortable or crosses the line in relationships. This self-awareness will empower you to express your needs confidently. Remember that setting boundaries is not about controlling others but about taking care of yourself emotionally.

When communicating boundaries, choose a time and place to have a calm and private conversation with the person involved. Use "I" statements to express your feelings and needs without blaming or accusing the other person. For example, say, "I feel overwhelmed when you make decisions for me without consulting me first" instead of "You always control everything." This approach helps prevent defensiveness and encourages understanding.

Consistency is critical when enforcing boundaries. Be prepared to reiterate your boundaries if they are not respected initially. It may take time for others to adjust to your new way of interacting, so be patient yet firm in upholding your limits. If someone repeatedly crosses your boundaries despite clear communication, consider evaluating the future of that relationship for your well-being.

In family dynamics, navigating boundary-setting can be particularly challenging due to long-standing patterns and expectations. It's important to remember that healthy relationships are built on mutual respect and consideration for each other's needs. Communicate with family members openly and honestly, emphasizing that setting boundaries is a positive step towards improving the relationship dynamics for everyone involved.

With friends and partners, establishing boundaries can lead to deeper connections based on trust and respect. Be open about your needs and listen attentively to theirs as well. Healthy relationships thrive on mutual understanding and support, which can only be achieved through effectively communicating boundaries.

Remember that setting boundaries is an act of self-care and self-respect. You create space for authentic connections built on mutual respect and emotional balance by clearly expressing your limits and expectations in relationships. Stay true to yourself, prioritize your well-being, and trust that healthy relationships will flourish when both parties honor each other's boundaries.

This section will delve into practical exercises designed to fortify your ability to establish and uphold boundaries in your relationships. By actively engaging with these exercises, you will gradually empower yourself to navigate interactions with a newfound sense of self-assuredness and clarity.

Exercise 1: Self-Reflection

Begin by setting aside dedicated time for self-reflection each day. Reflect on past interactions where you felt your boundaries were crossed or ignored. Identify patterns or triggers that led to these instances. Understanding the root causes can aid in setting more effective boundaries moving forward.

Exercise 2: Assertiveness Practice

Role-play scenarios with a trusted friend or therapist where you practice asserting your boundaries. Use "I" statements to express your needs clearly and confidently. The more you practice asserting yourself, the more natural it will become in real-life situations.

Exercise 3: Boundary-Setting Journal

Keep a boundary-setting journal where you record instances of successful boundary-setting as well as challenges faced. Reflect on how you felt before, during, and after asserting your boundaries. This journal can serve as a valuable tool for tracking progress and identifying areas for improvement.

Exercise 4: Visualization Techniques

Engage in visualization exercises where you imagine yourself confidently setting and upholding boundaries in various scenarios. Visualize yourself feeling empowered and respected when your boundaries are honored. This practice can help reinforce a positive mindset around boundary-setting.

Exercise 5: Setting Boundaries Gradually

Start by setting small boundaries in low-stakes situations before tackling more significant challenges. Gradually increasing the complexity of your boundaries will build your confidence over time. Remember, setting boundaries is a skill that improves with practice.

Exercise 6: Seeking Support

Don't hesitate to seek support from a therapist, support group, or trusted individual as you work on strengthening your boundary-setting skills. A supportive environment can guide you as you navigate this transformative process.

Exercise 7: Celebrating Progress

Acknowledge and celebrate each success, no matter how small. Recognize the courage it takes to assert your boundaries.

Celebrating your progress reinforces positive behaviour and motivates you to continue growing in this area.

By engaging wholeheartedly with these exercises, you are taking proactive steps towards reclaiming your autonomy and fostering healthier relationships based on mutual respect and understanding. Remember, establishing solid boundaries involves self-discovery and empowerment, leading to a liberated life free from codependency.

Boundaries are your new best friends. They are crucial tools for anyone striving to overcome codependency and build stronger, healthier relationships. Understanding the importance of setting and maintaining these boundaries is about knowing where to draw the line and respecting and valuing your emotional space.

Communication is key. When you learn effective ways to express your limits to family, friends, and partners, you empower yourself. Clear communication minimizes misunderstandings and builds a foundation of respect. It's important to remember that expressing your needs isn't selfish; it's a fundamental aspect of healthy relationships.

Practice makes perfect. The exercises designed in this chapter are tailored to strengthen your ability to uphold your newly set boundaries. Regular practice will boost your confidence and ensure these boundaries become a natural part of your daily interactions.

Remember, setting boundaries is a form of self-respect and self-care. It might initially feel uncomfortable, especially if you're used to putting others' needs before yours. However, with time and persistence, you'll find that boundaries bring balance and peace to your relationships.

Take control of your emotional well-being by actively applying the strategies discussed here. Each step you take is a move towards a more liberated life, free from the chains of codependency. You have the strength and the right to stand up for your emotional health. Embrace these changes with compassion for yourself, and watch as your relationships transform into sources of support and mutual respect.

As you continue on this journey, carry the lessons learned about the power of boundaries. They are not just barriers but bridges towards deeper connections with others and a more authentic relationship with yourself.

Chapter 5: The Power of No: Setting the Stage for Independence

"Independence is happiness."

Susan B. Anthony

Is "No" a Complete Sentence in Your Life?

When you find yourself routinely saying yes when you feel no, it signals that your boundaries might be blurred or non-existent. This is a common trait in codependent relationships, where the fear of displeasure or conflict overrides one's needs and desires. In this context, learning to say no is not just about refusing something; it's about affirming your right to prioritize your feelings and needs.

Recognizing the signs of codependency, such as a diminished

sense of self-identity and an excessive reliance on others for approval, is pivotal. Codependency can manifest in various ways—constantly seeking validation, feeling guilty for asserting oneself or putting another's needs consistently above one's own can be telltale signs. Addressing these patterns begins with understanding that assertiveness isn't selfishness; it's a form of self-respect.

The journey towards embracing assertiveness requires acknowledging its therapeutic benefits. It empowers individuals by validating their emotions and decisions without needing external approval. This affirmation of self can significantly boost self-esteem and reduce anxiety by establishing clear personal boundaries essential for healthy interpersonal relationships.

Implementing strategies to resist the urge for external validation involves practical steps. Start by identifying situations where you seek validation and consciously choose to rely on your judgment instead. This might initially feel uncomfortable, as discomfort is a natural part of growth and change. However, this process becomes more intuitive with practice, reinforcing a sense of independence and confidence.

Navigating the emotional landscape of becoming more self-assertive can be challenging. It often involves dealing with guilt or fear—emotions that might arise when setting boundaries. It's important during these times to remind yourself why these changes are necessary: they're not just about saying no to others but saying yes to a healthier, more autonomous you.

Practically speaking, start small. Practice assertiveness in low-stakes situations to build your confidence. For example, voicing a preference for a movie or a restaurant can be a preliminary step towards tackling more significant issues like making career choices or handling complex personal relationships without undue influence from others.

Lastly, remember that the path to greater self-assertiveness is a journey filled with learning and occasional setbacks. Embrace each step forward and recognize that each act of assertiveness is a building block towards a more liberated life. Engage actively with these strategies as exercises and integral parts of reshaping your relationship with yourself and others.

By adopting these approaches consistently, you empower yourself to lead a life defined not by the needs and approvals of others but by your authentic choices and desires.

Recognizing the therapeutic benefits of assertiveness is crucial in breaking free from the chains of codependency. Assertiveness empowers individuals to communicate their needs, set boundaries, and stand up for themselves healthily and respectfully. One can cultivate a sense of self-worth and autonomy by embracing assertiveness, which is essential in overcoming codependent behaviors. Learning to assert oneself allows for healthier relationships based on mutual respect and understanding.

To apply assertiveness effectively, it is essential to practice self-awareness and self-compassion. Understanding one's emotions, triggers, and needs is fundamental to expressing oneself assertively. Individuals can confidently communicate their thoughts and desires by acknowledging and validating their feelings without judgment. Moreover, practicing self-compassion enables individuals to treat themselves with kindness and understanding, fostering a positive self-image that supports assertive behavior.

Setting clear boundaries is another critical aspect of applying assertiveness in daily interactions. Establishing boundaries helps define personal limits and expectations in relationships, preventing others from infringing on one's emotional or physical well-being. By communicating boundaries assertively and consistently, individuals can protect their mental health and maintain a sense of autonomy within relationships. It is important to remember that setting boundaries is not selfish but a necessary self-care act.

Moreover, learning practical communication skills is vital in applying assertiveness successfully. Practicing active listening, using "I" statements to express feelings, and maintaining eye contact during conversations are essential components of assertive communication. By honing these skills, individuals can convey their thoughts and emotions clearly while respecting the perspectives of others.

Incorporating assertiveness into daily interactions may initially feel challenging for those accustomed to codependent patterns. However, with practice and persistence, individuals can gradually enhance their assertiveness skills and break free from codependency's grip. Embracing assertiveness fosters a sense of empowerment and self-respect, paving the way for healthier relationships built on equality and mutual understanding.

Resisting the Urge for External Validation: A Path to Self-Assertion and Independence

In the journey towards breaking free from the chains of codependency, one crucial aspect to address is the constant need for external validation. This need often stems from a lack of self-esteem and an overreliance on others for a sense of worth. Resisting this urge for external validation is a fundamental step towards reclaiming your independence and cultivating a healthier relationship with yourself.

One strategy to resist the urge for external validation is to focus on self-awareness. By becoming more attuned to your thoughts and emotions, you can start identifying when you seek validation from others. Mindfulness techniques can be beneficial, allowing you to observe your feelings without judgment and recognize patterns of seeking external approval.

Another effective strategy is to set boundaries. Establishing clear boundaries helps protect your emotional well-being and reduces the need for constant validation from others. Communicate assertively about your boundaries and prioritize your own needs and feelings. Remember that it is okay to say no when something doesn't align with your values or desires.

Practice self-validation regularly. Acknowledge your achievements, strengths, and progress without needing validation from external sources. Celebrate small victories, no matter how insignificant they seem, as they build a strong sense of self-worth that doesn't rely on others' opinions.

Shift your focus inward. Instead of seeking validation from external sources, redirect your attention towards self-care activities that nurture your well-being and boost your self-esteem. Engage in hobbies you enjoy, spend time with supportive friends and family, or seek professional help if needed to work through underlying issues contributing to codependent behaviors.

Challenge negative beliefs that fuel the need for external validation. Often, these beliefs are rooted in past experiences or societal expectations. Replace self-critical thoughts with positive affirmations, reminding yourself of your inherent worth and capabilities independent of others' opinions.

Find a support system that encourages your journey towards independence. Surround yourself with individuals who respect your boundaries, uplift you, and support your growth. Seek out therapy or support groups where you can connect with others who understand your struggles and provide valuable insights on overcoming codependency.

By employing these strategies to resist the urge for external validation, you empower yourself to break free from codependent patterns and embark on a path towards greater self-assertiveness and independence. Remember that others' approval does not determine your worth; it comes from within, waiting to be acknowledged and embraced by you.

Navigating the challenges and emotions tied to becoming more self-assertive can be a daunting task, especially for those who have been entrenched in codependent patterns. It's crucial to remember that the journey towards independence and self-assertiveness is a process, not an overnight transformation. As you embark on this path, expect resistance from within yourself and possibly from those around you who are accustomed to the old dynamics of your relationships.

One key strategy to navigate these challenges is setting boundaries. Boundaries are essential for establishing your sense of self and protecting your emotional well-being. Start by identifying what behaviors or interactions make you uncomfortable or compromise your values. Communicate your boundaries clearly and firmly, even if it feels uncomfortable initially. Remember that setting boundaries is an act of self-care, not selfishness.

Another vital aspect of becoming more self-assertive is practicing self-compassion. It's common to experience guilt or anxiety when asserting your needs and desires, especially if you've been conditioned to prioritize others over yourself. Remind yourself that prioritizing your well-being is acceptable and necessary for personal growth. Treat yourself with the same kindness and understanding that you would offer a close friend facing similar challenges.

As you navigate the emotional complexities of breaking free from codependency, remember that setbacks are a natural part of the process. Self-compassion also involves being gentle with yourself when faced with obstacles or moments of regression. Instead of berating yourself for perceived failures, view them as opportunities for learning and growth. Every step contributes to your journey towards independence, no matter how small.

Seeking support from trusted individuals or professionals can be instrumental in navigating the challenges of becoming more self-assertive. Surround yourself with people who respect and encourage your efforts towards personal growth. Therapy or counseling can provide valuable insights and tools to help you overcome deep-seated patterns of codependency. Embrace these resources as aids in your journey towards liberation from unhealthy relationship dynamics.

Practicing mindfulness can also aid in navigating the emotional terrain of developing self-assertiveness. Mindfulness lets you observe your thoughts and emotions without judgment, helping you better understand your inner world. By staying present in the moment, you can better discern your needs and respond assertively rather than reactively in challenging situations.

In summary, navigating the challenges and emotions of becoming more self-assertive requires patience, self-compassion, setting boundaries, seeking support, and practicing mindfulness. Embrace the process as an opportunity for personal growth and empowerment, knowing that each step towards independence brings you closer to living a liberated life free from codependency.

Empowering Your Journey Toward Independence

Assertiveness is not just a skill but a gateway to self-liberation. By understanding and embracing the therapeutic benefits of assertiveness, you equip yourself with the tools necessary to reclaim your identity and strengthen your self-esteem. Remember that being assertive means respecting both your needs and those of others, promoting healthier, more balanced relationships.

Resisting External Validation

The journey to overcome the need for external validation is both challenging and rewarding. By employing practical strategies such as setting personal goals and affirming your worth, you begin to trust in your intrinsic value. This shift significantly reduces anxiety and dependency on others for approval, paving the way for a more empowered and authentic life.

Navigating Emotional Challenges

Embracing assertiveness can stir a range of emotions, from fear to exhilaration. Recognizing these emotions as part of your growth process is vital. Equip yourself with coping mechanisms like mindfulness or seeking support from trusted individuals. These approaches help manage stress and fortify your resolve to maintain your newfound assertiveness.

Take Action

Every step you take towards being more self-assertive is a step away from codependency. Start small: practice saying "no" when it feels right, express your preferences openly, and set clear boundaries. Each action reinforces your sense of self and supports you in building a life where you are the priority.

Remember, breaking free from codependency doesn't happen overnight. But with consistent effort and dedication to applying these strategies, you can achieve lasting change in your relationships and, most importantly, within yourself. Embrace this journey with courage, knowing each step forward shapes a stronger, more independent you.

Chapter 6: Rediscovery: Cultivating Your Sense of Self

"We are all dependent on one another,

every soul of us on earth."

George Bernard Shaw

Are You Living Your Life, or Living for Others?

Rediscovering and cultivating your sense of self is perhaps the most empowering journey you can embark on, especially when breaking free from the chains of codependency. It's about shifting the focus to who you are, independent of your relationships and external validations. This chapter delves deeply into practical strategies that help you explore and strengthen your identity, fostering a robust sense of self-worth and integrating self-care practices into your daily life.

For many, codependency has masked their true identity, making it feel almost foreign to consider oneself outside the context of others. However, engaging in activities that allow for personal reflection is vital. These aren't just hobbies or pastimes but avenues to reconnect with your inner self. Whether it's art, writing, or solo sports, these activities serve as a mirror reflecting your most genuine parts to you.

Furthermore, cultivating a strong sense of self-worth is crucial. It's not uncommon for individuals struggling with codependency to feel a diminished sense of self-value. By setting achievable personal goals and celebrating each accomplishment, no matter how small, you begin to see yourself in a new light—one that shines based on your achievements and qualities rather than the approval of others.

Incorporating self-care practices into your daily routine is another transformative step. Self-care goes beyond mere pampering; it involves nurturing your body and mind to improve overall well-being. Regular exercise, balanced nutrition, adequate sleep, and mindfulness practices like meditation enhance your physical health and stabilize your emotional state, making you less dependent on external emotional support.

Empowerment comes from understanding that you control your emotional responses and life choices. This realization is liberating and forms the core of breaking free from codependency. Each step towards recognizing and affirming your needs is towards a healthier, more autonomous existence.

Remember, rediscovery isn't just about finding what was lost; it's about coming into new elements of yourself that were never given room to grow before. Each day provides growth and renewal opportunities—grab these opportunities with both hands!

By applying these insights, you create a life where *you* are at the center, not merely as a participant in someone else's orbit but as the master of your journey. This shift doesn't happen overnight but evolves through consistent practice and commitment to oneself.

Embrace this chapter as a guide to unlocking a more fulfilled and balanced life where relationships are an addition to, not the definition of, your happiness.

Engage in activities and reflections to explore personal identity beyond relationships. Begin this journey by setting aside time for self-discovery. Reflect on your interests, values, and aspirations independently of your relationships. Consider what brings you joy, what challenges you enjoy tackling, and what dreams you have for your future. By focusing on these aspects of yourself, you can unravel the layers of codependency that may have obscured your sense of self.

Dive into hobbies or activities that ignite your passion. Whether painting, hiking, cooking, or writing, immerse yourself in activities that bring you fulfillment and allow you to express your unique self. These pursuits can help you reconnect with your individuality and rediscover the parts of yourself that codependent relationships may have overshadowed.

Journal about your thoughts and feelings. Writing can be a powerful tool for self-reflection and exploration. Take time each day to jot down your thoughts, emotions, and observations about yourself. Use journaling to clarify your desires, fears, and goals outside your relationships.

Seek out new experiences and environments. Stepping outside of your comfort zone can be a catalyst for personal growth and self-discovery. Explore new places, try new activities, or engage with different communities to expand your perspective and learn more about yourself in diverse settings.

Connect with supportive friends or a therapist. Surround yourself with individuals who encourage your personal growth and validate your journey towards self-discovery. A therapist can provide guidance and support as you navigate the complexities of untangling codependent patterns and rediscovering your sense of self.

Cultivating Self-Worth and Independence: Keys to Breaking Free from Codependency

Fostering a strong sense of self-worth and independence is crucial in breaking free from codependency patterns. Self-worth forms the foundation of healthy relationships, as it influences how we allow others to treat us. To cultivate self-worth, begin by acknowledging your inherent value as an individual, separate from any relationships you may have. Recognize that your worth does not depend on external validation but stems from within yourself.

Independence is another crucial aspect to nurture. Embrace your ability to make decisions and take actions that align with your values and desires. Set boundaries that protect your well-being and honor your autonomy. Remember that it is healthy to prioritize your needs and desires alongside those of others.

Developing self-worth and independence involves practicing self-compassion. Treat yourself with the same kindness and understanding you would offer a close friend facing challenges. Celebrate your strengths and accomplishments, no matter how small they may seem. By acknowledging your worth and fostering independence, you pave the way for empowered relationships built on mutual respect and support.

Challenge negative self-talk that undermines your self-worth. Replace self-criticism with affirmations that highlight your strengths and capabilities. Recognize that you deserve love, respect, and fulfillment in all areas of life. Surround yourself with positive influences that uplift and validate your sense of self-worth.

Embrace self-discovery as an ongoing journey towards understanding yourself more deeply. Explore your interests, values, and passions outside of codependent dynamics. Engage in activities that bring you joy and fulfillment, independent of others' opinions or expectations. Investing in yourself and prioritizing your growth reinforces a strong sense of self-worth and independence.

Remember that building self-worth and independence takes time and practice. Be patient with yourself as you navigate this transformative process. Each small step towards embracing your worth and asserting your independence contributes to breaking free from codependency patterns, leading to healthier relationships based on mutual respect and authenticity.

Incorporating self-care practices into your daily routines enhances your self-perception and overall well-being. Self-care is not a luxury but a necessity, especially for individuals working to break free from codependency patterns. By prioritizing self-nurturing activities, you can cultivate a more profound sense of self-worth and resilience.

Start by setting boundaries in your life to protect your time and energy. Learn to say no to activities or people that drain you or do not align with your values. Respect your limits and honor your needs without guilt. This practice will reinforce your self-respect and empower you to make choices that serve your best interests.

Engage in activities that bring you joy and relaxation. Whether reading a book, walking in nature, practicing yoga, or indulging in a hobby, make time for things that nourish your soul. Nurturing yourself is not selfish; it's essential for your emotional well-being. When you prioritize self-care, you fill up your cup, making you better equipped to handle life's challenges.

Practice mindfulness to stay present and grounded in the moment. Mindfulness techniques such as deep breathing, meditation, or simply focusing on your senses can help reduce stress and anxiety while promoting inner peace. By being mindful, you can observe your thoughts and emotions without judgment, allowing yourself to respond thoughtfully rather than impulsively.

Connect with supportive individuals who uplift and encourage you on your journey towards self-discovery. Surround yourself with people who respect your boundaries, celebrate your successes, and offer a listening ear when needed. Healthy relationships are vital in fostering a positive self-image, reflecting the love and care you deserve.

Prioritize relaxation as part of your self-care routine. Adequate sleep is essential for both physical and mental health, allowing your body to recharge and rejuvenate. Create a bedtime ritual that promotes restful sleep, such as turning off electronic devices an hour before bed, dimming the lights, or practicing relaxation techniques like gentle stretching or reading a book.

Engage in physical activity that makes you feel good about yourself. Exercise releases endorphins, which are natural mood lifters, helping reduce feelings of stress and anxiety. Find an activity that resonates with you, whether dancing, hiking, swimming, or practicing yoga. Physical movement benefits your body and boosts your self-esteem by promoting a sense of accomplishment and vitality.

Incorporating these self-care practices into your daily life will enhance your self-perception and nurture a deeper connection with yourself. By valuing and prioritizing your well-being, you are breaking free from codependency patterns and embracing a more empowered way of living. Remember, self-care is an ongoing journey of self-discovery and self-love that requires commitment and dedication to nurturing the most critical relationship in your life—the one with yourself.

As we navigate the complexities of codependency, it becomes crucial to cultivate a robust sense of self. We take significant steps toward emotional independence and healthier relationships by engaging in activities that help explore our identity, foster self-worth, and incorporate self-care into our daily routines.

Engaging in self-exploration activities is more than just a pastime; it's essential for rediscovering who you are outside of your relationships. This is about finding hobbies and connecting deeply with your core values and desires. Each step in understanding yourself contributes to a stronger, more resilient identity.

Building self-worth cannot be overstated. Remember, your value does not decrease based on someone's inability to see your worth. By affirming your value independently, you empower yourself to make decisions that align with your best interests and not merely to please others.

Self-care practices are your daily reminders that you matter. They are not selfish; they are necessary. Integrating these practices helps improve not only how you view yourself but also how you interact with others. When you care for yourself, you signal to the world that your needs are essential and valid.

By taking these steps, you actively move away from codependent tendencies and embrace a life where your needs, desires, and happiness are prioritized. This shift enhances your life and sets a foundation for healthier, more balanced relationships.

Embrace these changes with patience and persistence. The journey towards breaking free from codependency is continuous and requires commitment. Each small step is a piece of the puzzle in reclaiming your autonomy and enriching your life.

Remember, every effort you make builds towards a liberated life where true fulfillment and happiness can flourish. Take charge of your journey with confidence and courage, knowing each step forward is a step towards a more empowered you.

Chapter 7: Emotional Alchemy: From Co-dependence to Co-empowerment

"Interdependence is and ought to be as much

the ideal of man as self-sufficiency.

Man is a social being."

Mahatma Gandhi

Transforming Codependency into Co-empowerment: A Journey Towards Emotional Freedom

In the realm of personal growth and healthy relationships,

breaking free from codependency represents a crucial pivot from relational dysfunction to mutual empowerment. This transformation is not merely about severing ties or creating emotional distance; it's about redefining the foundations upon which our relationships are built. At its core, the shift from codependence to co-empowerment involves a profound reevaluation of how we connect with others, ensuring these connections are rooted in respect, balance, and genuine interdependence.

The journey begins with a frank assessment of existing relationship dynamics. Often, those entangled in codependent relationships find themselves repeatedly sacrificing their own needs and desires to appease others, leading to a cycle of resentment and emotional imbalance. The path to empowerment necessitates challenging these patterns head-on, advocating for a relationship model where both parties contribute equally and healthily.

Setting clear boundaries is paramount. These boundaries aren't barriers meant to push others away but are decisive lines that protect our emotional well-being. They help delineate where one person ends and another begins, clarifying responsibilities and expectations. Through this clarification, individuals can avoid the common pitfall of overextending themselves emotionally or taking on burdens that aren't theirs to bear.

Prioritizing self-care emerges as another critical element in this transformative process. It involves nurturing oneself not out of selfishness but as a fundamental practice that enhances overall life quality and relational health. Engaging in self-care practices such as mindfulness, exercise, or simply allocating time for personal hobbies can rejuvenate one's spirit and foster sustained self-assurance.

This metamorphosis culminates in the cultivation of lasting self-empowerment. It requires individuals to confront deeply ingrained fears and self-doubt—often manifested from past traumas or dysfunctional family dynamics—and replace them with healthier beliefs and practices. This shift is not instantaneous but evolves through consistent effort and practical strategies to reinforce one's self-worth and capability.

Step-by-Step Guide: Crafting Emotional Equilibrium

Objective: To foster emotional balance within relationships through practical, actionable steps that encourage authenticity and mutual respect.

Step 1: Identify and Understand Your Emotions

Begin by becoming acutely aware of your emotional responses. Notice which situations trigger feelings of discomfort or happiness. Employ techniques like journaling or mindfulness to gain deeper insights into your emotional triggers and patterns.

Step 2: Validate Your Emotions

Acknowledge your feelings without judgment. Understand that it's perfectly natural to experience a wide range of emotions, and accepting them is a crucial step towards emotional maturity.

Step 3: Practice Emotional Self-Regulation

Develop personalized strategies for managing your emotions effectively. Whether it's through meditation, physical activities, or therapeutic conversations, find what helps you maintain emotional equilibrium.

Step 4: Communicate Emotions Effectively

Articulate your feelings using "I" statements that reflect your personal experiences rather than placing blame. Cultivate an environment where open communication is encouraged and respected.

Step 5: Set Healthy Emotional Boundaries

Define what you are willing to accept in your interactions with others. Establish limits that help you maintain a healthy emotional state without overextending yourself.

Step 6: Foster Authentic Connections

Seek out and nurture relationships that respect your emotional boundaries and where there is an equitable exchange of support and understanding.

By integrating these steps into daily life, individuals can transform previously codependent dynamics into relationships characterized by healthful interdependence. In this true emotional alchemy, mutual empowerment becomes the cornerstone of connection.

Breaking free from codependent relationships involves understanding the patterns that keep us trapped in unhealthy dynamics. It requires a deep dive into our behavior and beliefs to recognize how we may enable these patterns to continue. Setting clear boundaries is crucial in transforming codependent relationships into healthy, mutually respectful connections. Boundaries are essential for maintaining our sense of self and ensuring our needs are met without compromising our well-being.

To establish healthy boundaries, it is essential first to identify what behaviors and interactions make us uncomfortable or feel compromised. This self-awareness is critical to recognizing where we must draw lines in our relationships. Communicating these boundaries assertively and consistently is vital in shifting the dynamic from codependency to mutual respect. By setting and enforcing boundaries, we show others how we expect to be treated and create a foundation for healthier interactions.

In addition to boundaries, prioritizing self-care plays a significant role in breaking free from codependency. When prioritising our well-being, we tell ourselves and others that our needs matter. This can involve self-compassion, self-reflection, and engaging in activities that bring us joy and fulfillment. Self-care is not selfish but a fundamental aspect of maintaining emotional balance and cultivating self-empowerment.

Confronting our fears is another essential part of transforming codependent relationships. Fear often drives us to seek validation and security from others at the expense of our autonomy. By facing these fears head-on, we can unravel the insecurities that keep us tethered to unhealthy relationship patterns. Confronting fears empowers us to challenge limiting beliefs about ourselves and our worth, paving the way for greater emotional freedom.

Dismantling unhealthy beliefs about ourselves is a crucial step towards breaking free from codependency. Many individuals caught in codependent relationships harbor deep-seated beliefs of unworthiness or inadequacy, which perpetuate the cycle of seeking validation externally. Recognizing and challenging these beliefs allows us to reclaim our sense of self-worth and build confidence from within. Cultivating lasting self-assurance is a process that takes time and effort but is foundational in creating relationships based on equality and respect.

Cultivating Emotional Balance and Authenticity in Relationships

In navigating the complexities of relationships, fostering emotional balance and authenticity is paramount. It involves cultivating a deep self-awareness and understanding one's emotional responses to various situations. By honing this skill, individuals can navigate interactions more effectively, expressing their authentic selves while maintaining healthy boundaries. Authenticity in relationships requires a genuine connection with oneself, allowing for honest and open communication with others. This transparency fosters trust and mutual respect, laying the foundation for meaningful connections.

Emotional balance is a crucial aspect of nurturing healthy relationships. It entails constructively managing one's emotions avoiding reactive behaviors that may harm the relationship. Individuals can respond thoughtfully rather than impulsively by developing emotional intelligence, leading to more harmonious interactions. This balance allows for empathy and understanding towards others' feelings while honoring one's emotional needs.

Active listening is critical to fostering emotional balance and authenticity in relationships. By truly hearing and understanding the perspectives of others, individuals can cultivate deeper connections based on mutual respect and empathy. Active listening involves giving full attention to the speaker without judgment, allowing for genuine engagement and effective communication.

Setting boundaries is another essential aspect of maintaining emotional balance in relationships. Establishing clear boundaries communicates self-respect and asserts personal limits within the relationship dynamic. Communicating these boundaries openly and assertively is crucial, ensuring that both parties understand and respect each other's needs and limitations.

Self-care plays a vital role in nurturing emotional balance and authenticity within relationships. Prioritizing self-care practices such as regular exercise, mindfulness, adequate rest, and engaging in joyful activities can significantly impact one's emotional well-being. By taking care of oneself, individuals are better equipped to show up authentically in their relationships, fostering healthier connections based on mutual support and understanding.

Co-Empowerment Framework

A framework can serve as a guiding light in the transition from codependent relationships to co-empowered connections. This framework outlines the essential characteristics that define co-empowered relationships, fostering mutual respect, independence, balanced interactions, and transparent communication. Contrasting these attributes with codependent dynamics helps readers differentiate between unhealthy patterns and empowering behaviors. By providing concrete examples and relatable scenarios, individuals can better grasp the nuances of each type of relationship dynamic.

Characteristics of Co-Empowered Relationships

Mutual Respect: Co-empowered relationships thrive on a foundation of mutual respect. This entails valuing each other's opinions, boundaries, and autonomy. Both parties acknowledge and honor each other's individuality, creating a space where differences are celebrated rather than suppressed.

Independence: In co-empowered relationships, individuals maintain a sense of self-reliance and autonomy. Each person is responsible for their emotional well-being and personal growth, understanding that their partner complements rather than completes them.

Balanced Give-and-Take: Healthy relationships involve a balanced exchange of support, care, and resources. Co-empowered partners understand the importance of reciprocity, ensuring that both give and receive in equal measure without feeling depleted or overwhelmed.

Open Communication: Transparent communication forms the cornerstone of co-empowered relationships. Partners feel safe expressing their thoughts, feelings and needs openly and honestly without fear of judgment or rejection. This fosters trust and intimacy within the relationship.

Dynamics of the Co-Empowerment Model

The dynamics of the co-empowerment model emphasize

equilibrium through mutual collaboration and respect. Feedback loops are crucial in maintaining balance within the relationship, allowing for adjustments based on open communication and shared decision-making. Stability is achieved through a continuous process of self-awareness and mutual understanding.

Practical Implications

The co-empowerment framework equips individuals with practical tools to evaluate their relationships effectively. By using the provided checklist or criteria, readers can assess the health of their connections and identify areas for improvement towards co-empowerment. Action steps in the framework guide individuals in setting boundaries, articulating needs clearly, and fostering internal satisfaction independent of external validation.

Conclusion

In summary, cultivating relationships based on equal power dynamics requires a conscious effort to prioritize mutual respect, independence, balanced interactions, and open communication. The co-empowerment framework is a roadmap for individuals seeking to transform codependent patterns into healthy, fulfilling connections. By embracing these principles and taking proactive steps towards empowerment, readers can create relationships that nurture personal growth, emotional well-being, and lasting fulfillment.

Transforming codependent relationships into healthy,

empowering connections is possible but essential for personal growth and relational satisfaction. The journey from co-dependence to co-empowerment hinges on setting clear boundaries, fostering emotional balance, and nurturing interactions that thrive on mutual respect and equal power dynamics.

Understanding the mechanics of your relationships allows you to identify where dependencies may be limiting you and your loved ones. It's crucial to recognize these patterns early and with clarity. You initiate a powerful change that benefits everyone involved by challenging these dynamics. Remember, establishing boundaries is not about building walls between you and others; it's about clarifying your needs and expectations in a way that respects both your well-being and that of others.

Fostering emotional balance is about authenticity. It involves being truthful with yourself about your feelings and desires and expressing them in a way that is respectful and considerate. This authenticity builds trust and understanding in relationships, pillars of lasting connections.

Cultivating relationships based on equal power dynamics involves recognizing the value of each person's input and ensuring everyone feels heard and empowered. This can be achieved through active listening, shared decision-making, and a consistent practice of mutual support.

Embrace the empowerment from knowing you can transform relationships and enhance quality of life. Every step toward breaking old patterns is toward a more fulfilled self. Trust in your ability to change, lean on the resources available, and remember that you are not alone in this journey.

Take control of your relationship dynamics starting today. Engage actively with the strategies discussed, practice them daily, and watch your relationships transform into sources of strength and joy. Your efforts will improve your interpersonal connections and lead to a deeper understanding and love for yourself.

Chapter 8: Seeking Support: Therapy and Beyond

"If you want to go fast, go alone. If you

want to go far, go together."

African Proverb

Unlocking the Door to Recovery: The Power of Support in Conquering Codependency

The journey towards overcoming codependency often necessitates more than mere self-awareness and willpower; it requires robust support systems and strategic interventions. This realization brings us to the heart of structured therapeutic environments tailored to address the intricate web of codependent behaviors. Therapy, in its varied forms, serves not only as a refuge but as a proactive setting in which individuals can unearth the roots of their dependency, engage with personalized guidance, and cultivate effective coping strategies. The transformative potential of such therapeutic involvement is immense, offering recovery and a pathway to a liberated life.

Within the scope of therapeutic options, understanding the spectrum available is crucial. From traditional one-on-one sessions with psychologists specializing in addiction and relational issues to more contemporary group therapies and online support systems, each avenue offers unique benefits. These settings provide the confidentiality and safety necessary for individuals to express vulnerabilities and learn from others' experiences, fostering a collective journey towards healing.

Exploring these therapy options involves identifying professionals and programs that resonate on a personal level. This alignment is vital, as the therapeutic relationship is foundational to successful outcomes in codependency recovery. The efficacy of therapy hinges not only on professional expertise but also on the personal connection and trust developed between therapist and client.

Moreover, therapy for codependency extends beyond individual sessions. Group therapy and support groups present opportunities for peer support—spaces where individuals can share their struggles and successes without fear of judgment. These groups amplify the benefits of traditional therapy by embedding individuals within a community facing similar challenges.

Alternative support mechanisms also play a pivotal role in this expansive support system. Online forums, dedicated social media groups, and well-curated content provide ongoing resources accessible from anywhere. This continuous accessibility ensures that individuals are not isolated in their recovery journey; instead, they are continually supported by a network of peers and professionals.

Step-by-Step Guide: Crafting Your Recovery Tapestry

Step 1: Research Therapy Options

Begin by identifying therapists who specialize in areas relevant to codependency, such as addiction, trauma, or relational dynamics. Utilize online directories, read reviews, and perhaps most importantly, seek recommendations from trusted healthcare providers or peers who have embarked on similar therapeutic journeys.

Step 2: Schedule Initial Consultations

Arrange initial meetings with potential therapists to gauge compatibility. Prepare specific questions about their experience with codependency and their therapeutic approach. These initial consultations are crucial in selecting a therapist whose style and methodology align with your healing needs.

Step 3: Consider Group Therapy or Support Groups

Explore options for group therapy or specialized support groups focusing on codependency. These groups offer unique perspectives and communal support that can enhance personal insights and foster emotional resilience.

Step 4: Explore Online Resources

Find reputable online resources focusing on codependency recovery, including websites, blogs, forums, and social media platforms. Engaging with these resources can supplement your primary therapy work by providing additional insights and community support.

Step 5: Utilize Self-Help Books and Workbooks

Incorporate self-help books and workbooks into your recovery plan. Choose those with positive feedback from others who have found them beneficial. Actively engage with these materials to deepen your understanding of codependency and reinforce your daily practices towards recovery.

Step 6: Create a Supportive Network

Develop a supportive network of friends, family members, or mentors who understand the nature of codependency recovery. This network should provide encouragement, accountability, and non-judgmental listening—essential for sustainable recovery.

Step 7: Regularly Review and Adjust Your Support System

Continually assess the effectiveness of your chosen support strategies. Reflect on the most beneficial aspects and consider adjustments if certain elements do not meet your expectations or needs. This iterative process ensures your support system aligns with your evolving recovery journey.

Embracing these steps can significantly enhance one's ability to navigate the complexities of codependency recovery. Each component contributes uniquely to building a robust framework for sustained emotional health and relational autonomy—cornerstones of a truly liberated life.

Seeking support through therapy is a crucial step in addressing codependency. There are various therapy options available that can help individuals understand the roots of their codependent behaviors and develop healthier patterns. Individual therapy provides a one-on-one setting where individuals can explore their thoughts, emotions, and behaviors with a trained therapist. This personalized approach allows deep introspection and tailored guidance to address specific codependency issues.

Group therapy offers a supportive environment where individuals can connect with others facing similar challenges. It provides a sense of community and shared experiences, fostering empathy and understanding among participants. Group therapy can be particularly beneficial for those seeking validation and encouragement from peers while working on overcoming codependent behaviors.

Couples therapy, also known as relationship counseling, focuses on improving communication and dynamics within relationships affected by codependency. It helps couples identify unhealthy patterns, establish boundaries, and cultivate mutual respect. Couples therapy can be instrumental in fostering healthier connections based on trust, autonomy, and emotional intimacy.

Family therapy involves working with family members to address codependency issues that may have originated or been perpetuated within the family system. This therapy aims to improve communication, resolve conflicts, and promote understanding among family members. By exploring familial dynamics and generational patterns, individuals can gain insight into how their codependent behaviors developed.

Intensive therapy programs, such as residential treatment centers, provide immersive experiences for individuals seeking intensive support to address codependency. These programs offer round-the-clock care, therapeutic activities, and structured interventions to help individuals break free from entrenched patterns of codependency.

Exploring the Transformative Power of Codependency Therapy and Support

Seeking support through codependency therapy can be a transformative step towards breaking free from the chains of codependent behaviors. Therapy offers a safe and structured environment where individuals can explore the roots of their codependency, receive personalized guidance, and develop coping strategies to overcome these patterns. The benefits of codependency therapy are multifaceted, ranging from increased self-awareness to improved relationship dynamics.

In therapy, individuals can expect to delve deep into their past experiences and upbringing to understand how these have shaped their current behavior patterns. Therapists provide valuable insights into how codependency manifests in different aspects of life and guide clients in developing healthier coping mechanisms. Expect to work collaboratively with your therapist to set goals and track progress towards breaking free from codependency.

One of the critical benefits of codependency therapy is the opportunity for introspection and self-discovery. Through treatment, individuals can gain a better understanding of their own needs, boundaries, and emotions. Therapists help clients cultivate self-compassion and challenge negative beliefs that fuel codependent behaviors. This process empowers individuals to reclaim their sense of self-worth and autonomy.

Furthermore, codependency therapy equips individuals with

practical tools and strategies to navigate challenging situations in relationships. Therapists offer guidance on setting boundaries, communicating effectively, and prioritizing self-care. These skills are essential for establishing healthier relationships based on mutual respect and understanding.

In therapy, individuals can also expect validation for their experiences and emotions. Therapists create a non-judgmental space where clients can express themselves freely without fear of criticism or rejection. This validation is crucial for building confidence and self-esteem, often undermined by codependent relationships.

Overall, codependency therapy offers a holistic approach to healing from codependent behaviors by addressing underlying emotional wounds and fostering personal growth. Through treatment, individuals can journey toward self-discovery, empowerment, and authentic connection with others. The support provided in treatment is invaluable in navigating the complexities of overcoming codependency and building healthier relationships based on mutual respect and emotional well-being.

Support groups and online resources can provide valuable additional assistance for individuals navigating codependency. Support groups offer a safe space for individuals to share their experiences, gain insights from others facing similar challenges, and receive emotional support. These groups can be in-person or virtual, allowing for flexibility in participation. Engaging with a support group can help individuals realize that they are not alone in their struggles and that a community of people understands and empathises with their journey.

Online resources also significantly provide information, guidance, and tools for those seeking to break free from codependent patterns. Websites, forums, podcasts, and online courses dedicated to codependency offer a wealth of knowledge and strategies to empower individuals on their path to healing. These resources are easily accessible and can be utilized anytime, making them convenient for those with busy schedules or limited access to traditional therapy.

Joining a support group or exploring online resources can complement traditional therapy by offering continuous support between sessions. Peer support from others who have walked a similar path can be incredibly validating and inspiring. Additionally, online resources provide a wealth of information that individuals can explore at their own pace, deepening their understanding of codependency and the strategies for overcoming it.

In these spaces, individuals can find validation for their experiences and emotions, crucial in healing from codependency. The sense of community fostered by support groups and online platforms can help individuals build self-awareness and develop healthier coping mechanisms as they interact with others who share similar struggles. This shared journey towards healing can be immensely empowering and reassuring for those feeling overwhelmed by the challenges of codependency.

While therapy offers personalized guidance and structured sessions, support groups and online resources provide a more flexible approach to addressing codependency. They allow individuals to engage with the material at their own pace, connect with others outside of formal therapy settings, and access a variety of perspectives and insights from different sources. This diversity of input can enrich the healing process and offer individuals multiple avenues for growth and self-discovery.

By tapping into the collective wisdom of support groups and online resources, individuals can expand their understanding of codependency, learn new coping strategies, and feel supported on their journey towards liberation from unhealthy relationship dynamics. These alternative avenues offer complementary forms of assistance that enhance the effectiveness of traditional therapy, providing ongoing reinforcement and guidance as individuals work towards reclaiming their autonomy and well-being.

As we navigate the complex terrain of codependency, we must recognize that the journey towards healing and autonomy is not one to undertake alone. Exploring various therapy options provides a tailored approach that respects individual needs and circumstances. Each modality, from traditional psychotherapy to innovative online platforms, offers unique benefits that can significantly enhance one's ability to manage and eventually overcome codependent behaviors.

Therapy is a remedy and a transformational process that facilitates deep self-awareness and emotional growth. The structured environment of therapy sessions allows for the safe exploration of past patterns and gradually building new, healthier relationships with oneself and others. This support is invaluable, as it equips individuals with practical strategies and coping mechanisms essential for sustained recovery.

Moreover, alternative support avenues like support groups provide additional layers of communal healing. These platforms offer the comfort of shared experiences and the reassurance that one is not alone in their struggles. The collective wisdom found in such groups can often illuminate paths that may not have been visible in isolation.

Take proactive steps towards your recovery by engaging with these supportive networks. Whether through direct therapy or supplementary groups, embracing these resources can dramatically accelerate your progress towards a more balanced and fulfilling life. Remember, your journey is unique, so your healing process should also be. Leverage every available tool to craft a life defined not by codependency but by resilience and independence.

Embrace the courage to confront the challenges of codependency head-on. By doing so, you reclaim control over your emotional well-being and relationships. With each step forward, you pave the way for a life characterized by greater autonomy and healthier interdependence—where you are no longer surviving but thriving.

Chapter 9: The Company You Keep: Harnessing the Power of Support Groups

"The greatest gifts you can give your children are

the roots of responsibility and the

wings of independence."

Denis Waitley

Why Support Groups Can Be Your Most Powerful Ally in Overcoming Codependency

When embarking on overcoming codependency, it's essential to recognize that this is not a path to walk alone. The complexities of codependent behaviors often stem from deeply rooted patterns linked to our relationships and self-perception. Community and support play pivotal roles in unraveling these patterns, offering strength and perspective that are hard to find in isolation.

Engaging with support groups can significantly enhance your healing process. These groups provide a platform where experiences are shared openly, free from judgment, fostering an environment of understanding and empathy. Here, you are heard and validated, which is crucial for anyone struggling with the feelings of inadequacy that often accompany codependent relationships.

Learning how to engage with these groups effectively can make all the difference. It's not merely about attendance; it's about active participation and the willingness to be vulnerable. By sharing your experiences and listening to others, you gain insights often obscured by personal biases or pain. This reciprocal exchange doesn't just bolster your emotional toolkit—it helps reshape your interpersonal dynamics and self image.

Moreover, support groups help you recognize patterns and triggers in a controlled environment, enabling you to practice new behaviors like setting boundaries or communicating assertively in a safe space. These rehearsals are invaluable; they empower you with the confidence to apply new skills in real-world interactions, essential for breaking the cycles of codependency.

The benefits of support groups extend beyond learning opportunities and provide a consistent reminder that you're not alone in this struggle. The sense of belonging can significantly reduce the loneliness and isolation that many feel when dealing with codependent relationships. This solidarity is vital as it reinforces the shared human experience, reminding us that we all have struggles and are more resilient as a community.

To maximize these benefits, it's essential to choose the right group. Look for one that aligns with your specific needs and values, ensuring a match in the group's focus and its members' attitudes. A supportive, positive group dynamic is crucial as it enhances everyone's ability to grow.

In sum, while the road to overcoming codependency may be challenging, incorporating support groups into your recovery strategy can provide powerful reinforcement. These groups offer more than just advice—they give a mirror showing us who we can become when we break free from old patterns and embrace new ways of relating to ourselves and others. Engage actively, share bravely, and watch as you transform within the camaraderie of those who truly understand.

Recognizing the Importance of Community in the Healing Process

Healing from codependency is a journey that often requires more than just individual effort. The importance of community in this process cannot be overstated. Support groups provide a safe space for individuals to share their experiences, gain valuable insights, and receive encouragement from others who have walked similar paths. Being part of a supportive community can offer a sense of belonging and validation, essential for rebuilding self-esteem and breaking free from unhealthy relationship patterns.

Engaging with a community of like-minded individuals can help combat feelings of isolation often accompanying codependency. It offers an opportunity to connect with others who understand your challenges and can provide empathy and understanding without judgment. Feeling understood and accepted is crucial in fostering healing and growth, as it creates a foundation of trust that allows for vulnerability and authentic self-expression.

Support groups also serve as a source of accountability, gently guiding individuals towards positive change by providing feedback, encouragement, and constructive criticism when needed. Being surrounded by peers committed to personal growth can inspire motivation and determination to overcome obstacles and change behavior and thought patterns.

Moreover, community support can provide valuable resources such as information, tools, and strategies for managing codependent tendencies effectively. Learning from others' experiences and successes can offer new perspectives and insights that may not have been considered otherwise. By tapping into the group's collective wisdom, individuals can accelerate their healing process and make significant strides towards breaking free from codependency.

Embracing the Power of Support Groups in Overcoming Codependency

Support groups can be invaluable resources for individuals on the path to overcoming codependency. These groups offer a safe space where individuals can share their experiences, receive support, and gain insights from others facing similar challenges. Engaging with support groups can provide a sense of community and belonging, which is crucial for healing and growth. It allows individuals to realize that they are not alone in their struggles and that others understand what they are going through.

When participating in support groups, it is essential to approach them with an open mind and a willingness to learn. Being receptive to feedback and different perspectives can lead to profound personal growth. It is also essential to actively participate in discussions, share your thoughts and feelings honestly, and listen attentively to others. By engaging fully in the group process, you can maximize the benefits of being part of a supportive community.

Setting realistic expectations for what you hope to gain from the support group is vital. Understand that healing is a gradual process that takes time and effort. Be patient with yourself and trust in the journey of self-discovery and emotional healing. Support groups can provide valuable tools, strategies, and coping mechanisms that can aid you on your path toward breaking free from codependent patterns.

In support groups, it is expected to encounter individuals at different stages of their healing journey. Learning from those who have made progress can offer hope and inspiration, while offering guidance to those earlier in their process can be empowering. The group's diverse experiences foster a rich learning and personal development environment.

Building connections with fellow group members outside of meetings can further enhance the sense of community and support. Engaging in activities, sharing resources, or simply checking in with one another can strengthen bonds and create a network of encouragement. These connections can be instrumental in maintaining motivation and momentum on your path toward liberation from codependency.

Remember that each individual's journey is unique, and progress may not always follow a linear path. Be kind to yourself during setbacks or moments of struggle, knowing they are part of the growth process. Embrace the support the group offers as a source of strength during challenging times, allowing yourself to lean on others when needed.

In a safe and supportive environment, sharing personal experiences and insights can be incredibly empowering for those on the journey of overcoming codependency. By opening up and expressing your thoughts, feelings, and struggles, you validate your experiences and create a space for others to relate and offer support. This exchange of stories can foster a sense of belonging and understanding, showing that you are not alone in your struggles.

When sharing in a group setting, being authentic and vulnerable is essential. Honesty and openness can pave the way for deep connections with others who may be going through similar challenges. By letting down your guard, you can receive empathy, compassion, and valuable insights from those who genuinely want to see you grow and heal.

Listening to the experiences of others can also be enlightening and validating. Being an attentive listener shows respect for others' journeys and allows you to gain new perspectives on your struggles. You may find solace in realizing that many others share similar feelings and experiences, which can be reassuring in breaking down the walls of isolation that often accompany codependency.

Participating in a supportive group environment offers a sense of camaraderie that is essential for emotional healing. Feeling understood by those who have walked a similar path can provide a sense of validation and acceptance crucial in building self-worth independent of external validation. These connections can also serve as a source of motivation, encouragement, and accountability as you break free from codependent patterns.

Sharing personal experiences in a safe space allows for emotional release and catharsis. Expressing your emotions without judgment can be incredibly liberating and healing. It will enable you to process complicated feelings, gain clarity on your thoughts, and release pent-up emotions that may have held you back.

Engaging with others in a supportive setting also provides opportunities to learn new coping strategies, gain valuable insights, and receive constructive feedback. By being open to different perspectives and approaches, you can expand your toolkit for navigating challenging situations and fostering healthier relationships.

In essence, sharing personal experiences and insights within a supportive group setting is an integral part of the healing journey from codependency. It offers connection, validation, growth, and emotional release, which are crucial in breaking free from unhealthy relationship patterns. Embrace the power of community as you continue on your path towards self-discovery, healing, and empowerment.

As we navigate the complexities of overcoming codependency, the significance of community and support groups cannot be overstated. These groups provide a crucial platform for self-reflection and offer a structured environment where you can practice setting boundaries and assertive communication. They are about sharing struggles and building the frameworks for healthier relationships and a stronger sense of self.

Engaging with support groups effectively means being active in your participation. It involves more than just attendance; it requires involvement, openness, and the willingness to give and receive advice. This proactive engagement is essential as it fosters a deeper understanding of personal experiences and insights, enhancing the healing process.

Sharing your journey in a safe and supportive environment is invaluable. It allows you to hear others' stories that may mirror your own, providing reassurance that you are not alone in this battle. These narratives can serve as powerful reminders of the progress possible through persistence and the supportive hand of a community.

To truly benefit from these groups, embrace them as a resource for emotional growth and learning. Let them guide you in developing healthier interpersonal dynamics and cultivating a robust sense of individuality, free from the need for external validation.

Remember, the path to overcoming codependency is one you need not walk alone. Support groups offer a compass and companionship on this journey, helping to illuminate the way forward with hope and empowerment. Embrace these communities as vital allies in pursuing liberation from codependent behaviors, encouraging you to live a life defined by self-love and mutual respect.

Chapter 10: Embarking on the Path to Recovery

"To find yourself, think for yourself."

Socrates

A New Dawn in Codependency Recovery: Embracing the Journey Together

When you begin to confront and manage codependency, it can feel like stepping onto a path shrouded in fog. The direction might be unclear, and the destination seems far away. However, support groups tailored explicitly for those dealing with codependency offer a beacon of light, providing both direction and companionship on this journey towards recovery. These groups are not just a meeting point but a vital resource that fosters growth, resilience, and mutual support.

The strength of these groups lies in their ability to create a safe space where individuals can share experiences without judgment. Here, every story matters, and every small victory is celebrated. Participants are encouraged to map out their recovery journey by setting achievable milestones. This structured approach helps recognize each step forward, no matter how small. It's crucial to understand that recovery is not linear; it involves ups and downs, successes and setbacks.

In dealing with these inevitable challenges, developing effective coping mechanisms is vital. Support groups often facilitate skill-building sessions where members can learn and practice new strategies for handling stress, avoiding triggers, and maintaining emotional balance. These skills are vital in overcoming codependency and invaluable in various aspects of life.

Another pivotal aspect of these groups is the celebration of achievements. Recognizing and honoring the progress made by members is a powerful motivator and reinforces the value of the journey. Celebrations help lift the group's spirit, boosting confidence and inspiring others to persevere through their struggles.

Furthermore, these settings provide an opportunity to witness real-life transformations—seeing peers evolve into more independent and self-assured individuals can be incredibly inspiring. It serves as a tangible reminder that change is possible, encouraging others to continue forging their paths towards independence.

What makes support groups especially effective is their foundation of shared experiences. Knowing that others have faced similar challenges—either overcome or are currently battling them—creates a sense of solidarity that is hard to find elsewhere. This communal understanding helps mitigate feelings of isolation or uniqueness often accompanying codependency issues.

Lastly, an essential benefit of participating in such groups is gaining access to a network of ongoing support. Recovery from codependency doesn't end with the conclusion of a session; it's a continuous process that requires persistence and dedication. Access to a supportive community ensures that help is always available when challenges arise outside the structured environment of regular meetings.

Embarking on this path may be difficult, but joining a support group can make the journey less daunting. By mapping out your recovery path, developing robust coping mechanisms, celebrating every achievement, and leaning on a community for support, you set the stage for lasting change and personal growth.

As you begin your journey towards recovery from codependency, it is essential to map out a clear path with achievable milestones and markers to track your progress. Setting specific goals can help you stay focused and motivated on the road to healing and self-discovery. By breaking down your recovery journey into manageable steps, you can create a sense of direction and purpose in your efforts to break free from codependent patterns.

Start by identifying areas in your life where codependency has significantly impacted. Whether in your relationships with others, your sense of self-worth, or your ability to set boundaries, pinpointing these areas will allow you to target them effectively in your recovery process. Acknowledging the effects of codependency is the first step towards reclaiming control over your life and relationships.

Next, establish realistic milestones that align with your long-term recovery goals. These milestones could be as simple as setting boundaries with a loved one, practicing self-care regularly, or seeking therapy to address underlying issues. By breaking down larger objectives into smaller, achievable steps, you can build momentum and celebrate each milestone as a victory on your path to healing.

Recognize and celebrate your progress along the way. Acknowledging your small wins and improvements as you work towards overcoming codependency is essential. Celebrating these moments of growth can boost your confidence and motivation, reinforcing your commitment to change.

Stay flexible in adapting your milestones as needed. Recovery is not always linear, and setbacks may occur along the way. Being open to adjusting your goals and strategies based on new insights or challenges will help you navigate the ups and downs of the recovery journey with resilience and determination.

Cultivating Coping Mechanisms for Codependency Recovery

Navigating the path to recovery from codependency involves developing coping mechanisms to handle setbacks and challenges along the way. It's essential to recognize that setbacks are a natural part of the healing process and do not diminish your progress. Embracing resilience and adaptability is critical to overcoming these hurdles.

One effective coping mechanism is to practice self-compassion. Treating yourself with kindness and understanding is crucial when faced with challenges or setbacks. Acknowledge your feelings without judgment and remind yourself that it's sometimes okay to struggle. Self-compassion allows you to nurture a positive relationship with yourself, fostering inner strength and self-acceptance.

Another valuable strategy is to seek support from your codependency support group or therapist. Connecting with others who understand your experiences can provide comfort, guidance, and perspective. Share your struggles openly within these safe spaces, allowing yourself to receive empathy and encouragement from those who genuinely care about your well-being.

Practice mindfulness to stay grounded in the present moment. Mindfulness techniques can help you manage stress, anxiety, and overwhelming emotions effectively. By focusing on the here and now, you can cultivate a sense of calmness and clarity amidst challenging situations, enabling you to respond thoughtfully rather than impulsively.

Set healthy boundaries to protect your emotional well-being. Establishing clear boundaries in your relationships helps you maintain a sense of autonomy and self-respect. Communicate your needs assertively and prioritize self-care without feeling guilty for putting yourself first.

Engage in activities that bring you joy and relaxation. Taking time for hobbies, exercise, or creative pursuits can help alleviate stress and boost mood. Nurturing your passions outside of codependent dynamics fosters a sense of individuality, reminding you of the unique qualities that make you who you are beyond your relationships.

Practice gratitude to cultivate a positive mindset. Acknowledging the blessings in your life, no matter how small, can shift your focus from difficulties towards moments of joy and appreciation. Gratitude is a powerful tool for resilience, helping you navigate challenges with a hopeful outlook.

Incorporating these coping mechanisms into your daily routine can strengthen your emotional resilience and empower you to face setbacks with courage and determination. Remember that recovery is a journey filled with ups and downs, but each challenge overcome brings you closer to liberation from codependency's chains.

As you celebrate your achievements and witness the transformation into a more independent self, you must acknowledge your progress on your journey towards breaking free from codependency. Each step taken, no matter how small it may seem, is a significant milestone in your recovery process. Recognize and honor your growth, which signifies your dedication to personal development and the courage to confront challenging patterns.

Embrace the positive changes you have experienced along the way. Whether setting healthier boundaries, asserting your needs, or fostering self-compassion, these shifts demonstrate your commitment to creating a more fulfilling and balanced life. Celebrate these victories, no matter how minor they appear, as they collectively contribute to your overall progress.

Reflect on the moments of empowerment you have encountered throughout your journey. Recognize when you stood up for yourself, prioritized self-care, or challenged limiting beliefs. These instances highlight your inner strength and resilience, showcasing your ability to navigate difficulties with grace and determination.

Share your achievements with others who support your recovery journey. Whether it's a trusted friend, therapist, or fellow group member, discussing your successes can amplify their impact and reinforce your commitment to change. Seek validation and encouragement from those who understand your challenges, as their insights can provide valuable perspective and motivation.

As you evolve into a more independent self, cultivate a sense of gratitude for your progress. Acknowledge the obstacles you have overcome and the growth stemming from these experiences. Express appreciation for your resilience in facing adversity and embracing transformation, recognizing the strength within you that propels you forward.

Stay committed to your recovery journey, even when faced with setbacks or challenges. Remember that growth is not always linear, and setbacks are opportunities for learning and development. Approach obstacles with resilience and a mindset focused on solutions rather than dwelling on difficulties.

In celebrating your achievements and embracing your evolving sense of self, remember that transformation is an ongoing process. Continue to nurture yourself, prioritize self-discovery, and cultivate relationships that support your well-being. Embrace the journey of personal growth with openness and curiosity, knowing that each step forward brings you closer to living a liberated life free from codependency's chains.

Embarking on the path to recovery from codependency is a courageous step toward self-liberation and healthier relationships. You establish a structured path that fosters progress and clarity by mapping out your recovery journey with clear, achievable milestones. This practical approach helps visualise your goals and track your achievements, no matter how small they may seem.

Developing effective coping mechanisms is crucial, as setbacks are inevitable in any recovery process. Embrace these challenges as opportunities for growth. Equip yourself with strategies such as reaching out to support groups, practicing mindfulness, or seeking professional guidance when faced with obstacles. Remember, every challenge you overcome is a testament to your resilience and commitment to self-improvement.

Moreover, it's essential to celebrate your achievements throughout this journey. Acknowledging and rejoicing in these victories enhances your motivation and reaffirms your belief in your ability to change. Celebrations can be simple, like taking time or sharing your progress with supportive friends or family members.

The role of codependency support groups cannot be overstated. These groups provide a platform where empathy, experiences, and encouragement flow freely among those who truly understand what you are going through. They offer both support and practical advice that can be crucial in navigating the complexities of recovery.

Take control of your life by actively engaging with these strategies. Your journey towards a more independent and fulfilling life is within reach—step by step, daily. Harness the power of community support, recognize your progress, face challenges boldly, and celebrate every step forward. You are capable of breaking free from the chains of codependency and transforming not only your relationships but also yourself.

Chapter 11: Life Beyond Codependency: Navigating New Relationships

"No man is an island, no man stands alone."

Dionne Warwick

Are You Ready for a Relationship Revolution?

Embarking on new relationships after experiencing codependency can feel like navigating uncharted waters. This journey, while daunting, offers a transformative path toward self-discovery and relational fulfillment. The insights from leading resources on overcoming codependency give you the tools to venture into new relationships and thrive.

This exploration focuses squarely on empowering you to enter new relationships with clarity and confidence. Understanding your own needs and desires is pivotal. It's about building a foundation where your sense of self is neither overshadowed nor undermined by others. This preparation involves recognizing personal patterns that previously led to codependent behaviors and actively working to shift these patterns in a healthier direction.

The next crucial step is applying your knowledge to maintain healthy dynamics in future relationships. It's not just about avoiding past mistakes; it's about fostering a proactive approach to relationship health. This means communicating openly, setting boundaries respectfully, and ensuring mutual understanding and respect are at the core of all interactions.

One of the most empowering tools is learning to set and respect boundaries. Boundaries help define your limits and how much you are willing to give and receive in a relationship. This isn't just about saying no; it's about saying yes to a more balanced, fulfilling partnership.

Moreover, every new relationship is an opportunity to apply self-awareness in fresh contexts. This involves being mindful of your emotional responses and triggers in interactions with others. Self-awareness allows you to navigate these interactions without returning to old, destructive habits.

Recognizing that setbacks are part of the learning curve is also vital. Each relationship will test your resolve and the integrity of your newfound boundaries and self-awareness practices. However, viewing these as opportunities for growth rather than failures can transform potential setbacks into powerful learning moments.

Lastly, remember that this journey is as much about discovering who you are concerning others as it is about forming or reforming connections with them. Every step forward in this journey adds a layer of strength and understanding to your character, contributing profoundly to both personal happiness and relationship satisfaction.

By embracing these strategies, you equip yourself for survival without codependency and thriving in every aspect of life. The transition into new relational dynamics doesn't signify the end of challenges but heralds a period of greater emotional autonomy and healthier interpersonal engagements.

Navigating new relationships after breaking free from codependency can be both exciting and daunting. It marks a fresh beginning, a chance to redefine how you interact with others and, most importantly, with yourself. As you prepare to enter this new phase of your life, it's crucial to approach it with confidence and a clear sense of self. Building a solid foundation within yourself is critical to forming healthy connections with others. Take the time to reflect on your values, boundaries, and what truly matters to you in a relationship.

Self-awareness is your greatest asset. Understand your triggers, fears, and desires to communicate them effectively with potential partners. Recognize your worth and believe you deserve relationships that uplift and support you. Setting boundaries is not a sign of weakness but of strength. Clearly define what is acceptable and not in your interactions with others.

Practice self-care regularly. Prioritize activities that nurture your mind, body, and spirit. Engage in hobbies that bring you joy, spend time with supportive friends and family, and invest in your well-being. When you care for yourself, you are better equipped to engage authentically in relationships.

As you establish new relationships, remember that your past experiences do not define you. Each interaction is an opportunity for growth and learning. Embrace the chance to connect with others from a place of authenticity and self-assurance. Trust in your ability to navigate these new waters with grace.

Maintaining Healthy Dynamics in Future Relationships

After a deeper understanding of codependency and learning to break free from unhealthy relationship patterns, applying this newfound knowledge to maintain healthy dynamics in future relationships is essential. Implementing boundaries is crucial in ensuring you do not fall back into codependent behaviors. By clearly defining what is acceptable and unacceptable in your relationships, you establish a foundation of respect for yourself and others.

Communication plays a pivotal role in maintaining healthy relationships. Expressing your needs, feelings, and concerns openly and honestly fosters understanding between you and your partner. Effective communication also involves active listening, allowing you to comprehend your partner's perspective without judgment or assumptions.

Self-care is not selfish but a fundamental aspect of nurturing healthy relationships. Prioritizing your well-being by setting aside time for activities that bring you joy and relaxation strengthens your self-worth. Caring for yourself makes you better equipped to contribute positively to your relationships.

Embrace vulnerability as a strength rather than a weakness. Being vulnerable with your partner by sharing your fears, insecurities, and desires creates a more profound connection based on authenticity and trust. Vulnerability fosters emotional intimacy, leading to more meaningful and fulfilling relationships.

Practice forgiveness as part of maintaining healthy relationships. Holding onto grudges or resentment can poison the dynamics between you and your partner. Forgiveness does not mean condoning harmful behavior but instead releasing yourself from anger and resentment, allowing space for healing and growth.

Cultivate gratitude in your relationships by acknowledging and appreciating the positive aspects of your partner. Expressing gratitude fosters a sense of mutual respect and appreciation, strengthening your bond. Recognizing the value your partner brings to your life enhances the quality of your relationship.

Continuously reflect on your growth within the relationship. Self-awareness is crucial in maintaining healthy dynamics, as it allows you to recognize any patterns or behaviors that may be detrimental to the relationship. Regularly assessing your progress and areas for improvement enables personal growth and strengthens the connection with your partner.

By applying these strategies, you can navigate new relationships confidently and clearly, building solid foundations based on mutual respect, communication, and self-awareness. Remember that maintaining healthy dynamics requires ongoing effort and commitment from both partners, but the rewards of cultivating fulfilling relationships are immeasurable.

In navigating new relationships beyond codependency, it is crucial to understand the importance of applying boundaries and self-awareness in these fresh contexts. Setting boundaries is a fundamental aspect of cultivating healthy relationships. It involves communicating your needs, limits, and expectations clearly to others. Establishing boundaries protects your emotional well-being and ensures relationships are based on mutual respect and understanding.

Self-awareness plays a significant role in developing fulfilling connections with others. Self-awareness allows you to recognize your emotions, thoughts, and behaviors, leading to a deeper understanding of yourself and how you interact with those around you. Through self-awareness, you can identify patterns from past codependent relationships and make conscious choices to avoid falling back into unhealthy dynamics.

When entering new relationships, taking time to reflect on your values, desires, and personal boundaries is essential. Understanding what you need and want from a relationship enables you to communicate effectively with potential partners and establish a strong foundation of honesty and authenticity. Honest communication is vital in setting clear boundaries and expressing your needs without fear or hesitation.

Moreover, practicing self-compassion is crucial as you navigate new relationships. Be kind to yourself and acknowledge that growth takes time and effort. Mistakes may happen along the way, but viewing them as learning opportunities rather than failures can help you continue toward healthier connections.

In new contexts, it is vital to stay true to yourself and not compromise your values or boundaries for the sake of a relationship. Healthy relationships are built on mutual respect and understanding, where both individuals feel free to express themselves authentically without fear of judgment or manipulation.

Regular self-check-ins are beneficial in maintaining awareness of your emotions and behaviors within a new relationship. Take time to assess your feelings, whether your boundaries are respected, and whether the dynamic feels healthy and balanced. This practice allows you to make adjustments as needed to ensure that you are prioritizing your well-being.

Lastly, seek support from trusted friends, family members, or a therapist as you navigate new relationships post-codependency. A supportive network can guide, validate, and encourage you as you progress towards healthier relationship patterns. Remember that growth is a process, and each step taken towards self-empowerment and independence is a significant achievement in breaking free from codependency's chains.

As we wrap up this discussion on forging ahead into new relationships after breaking free from codependent patterns, it's crucial to highlight the transformative journey you are embarking on. Embracing your newfound confidence and a clear sense of self will prepare you for future relationships and ensure they are healthy and fulfilling.

Confidence and a clear sense of self are foundational when entering new interactions. Remember, the relationship with yourself sets the tone for every other relationship you have. It's essential to nurture this primary connection, ensuring you're entering new relationships not out of need but from a place of wholeness.

In maintaining healthy dynamics in future relationships, the learning you've applied from overcoming codependency becomes invaluable. This isn't just about avoiding past pitfalls but actively creating a balanced, respectful, and nurturing environment for all involved. Each interaction allows you to practice these dynamics, reinforcing your growth and understanding.

Applying boundaries and self-awareness in new contexts might initially seem challenging, but it's a decisive step towards lasting personal empowerment. Boundaries aren't barriers; they are your guidelines that help others understand how to engage with you respectfully and lovingly. Coupled with self-awareness, boundaries ensure your relationships are genuinely supportive and enriching.

Take control of your emotional narrative. You have the tools and insights to navigate through these new territories effectively. Engage actively with what you've learned about yourself, your needs, and your values. Each step forward is a reinforcement of your independence and strength.

Let each relationship reflect your growth rather than your past constraints. You possess the innate ability to create connections that are not only healthy but also uplifting and affirming. With each positive interaction, you reaffirm your journey towards a liberated life with abundant joy, respect, and mutual support.

Now is the time to embrace these changes with open arms and heart. Your path to enriched relationships is clear; walk it confidently, purposefully, and joyfully.

Chapter 12: The Healing Workbook: Your Roadmap to Recovery

"Only in growth, reform, and change, paradoxically enough, is true security to be found."

Anne Morrow Lindbergh

Unlock the Power of Self-Healing

Taking control of your healing journey is a formidable yet profoundly rewarding task. For those entangled in the webs of codependency, the path to recovery can sometimes seem daunting and obscure. This is where a structured, well-designed workbook tailored for codependency recovery becomes invaluable. By guiding you through practical exercises, this workbook aims to empower you with the skills to reclaim your autonomy and enhance your emotional resilience.

Practical exercises are at the heart of this approach. Each exercise has been carefully crafted to help you understand the roots of codependent behaviors and provide actionable steps toward personal growth. These activities serve as stepping stones that gradually lead you out of habitual patterns and into a space where you can act independently and healthily in relationships.

The workbook also emphasizes the importance of identifying and challenging codependent thoughts. Through various reflective questions and scenarios, you are encouraged to examine the narratives you hold about yourself and your relationships. This critical examination is crucial because it lays the groundwork for transforming thought patterns that have long perpetuated codependent dynamics.

Equally important is the workbook's role in helping you track progress and reflect on your development. Regular check-ins via journal prompts or self-assessment tools allow you to see how far you've come in your journey. This motivates continued effort and helps solidify the new learning and behaviors as part of your everyday life.

Navigating these exercises, you'll find that each page is designed with knowledge, compassion and understanding. It acknowledges the struggles uniquely faced by those overcoming codependency while providing a clear, practical roadmap towards emotional independence.

By engaging actively with the workbook, you're not just reading about recovery but practicing it. This hands-on approach ensures that the concepts learned are understood and applied, fundamentally changing how you relate with yourself and others.

The journey through codependency to liberated living is deeply personal yet universally challenging. It requires courage, commitment, and, most importantly, a reliable guide. This workbook offers just that—a guide that walks beside you, offering clarity and support as you untangle old habits and forge new, healthier ways of being.

Remember, every page turned is a step closer to a more empowered self who can stand independently while connecting deeply and healthily with others. Embrace this process with an open heart and mind, ready to transform challenges into stepping stones for growth.

In your journey towards healing from codependency, practical exercises from workbooks can be invaluable tools for personal growth. These exercises help you develop self-awareness, set boundaries, and build emotional resilience. By engaging with the activities in a codependency workbook, you can actively work towards breaking free from destructive patterns and fostering healthier relationships with yourself and others.

One essential aspect of utilizing a codependency workbook is its opportunity for introspection and reflection. Through guided exercises, you can delve into your thoughts, emotions, and behaviors to better understand the root causes of your codependent tendencies. This self-awareness is crucial for initiating meaningful change and fostering personal growth.

Setting boundaries is another key focus of many codependency workbooks. By practicing boundary-setting exercises, you can learn to assert your needs and prioritize your well-being without feeling guilty or responsible for others' emotions or actions. Establishing healthy boundaries is fundamental in breaking free from codependency and cultivating more balanced relationships.

Moreover, codependency workbooks often include activities that promote emotional resilience. These exercises help you develop coping strategies, self-soothing techniques, and effective stress and anxiety management methods. Building emotional resilience equips you with the tools necessary to navigate challenging situations more efficiently and maintain stability in your emotional well-being.

As you engage with the practical exercises in a codependency workbook, remember that progress is not always linear. It's normal to encounter setbacks or challenges along the way. The key is approaching these obstacles with compassion and perseverance, viewing them as opportunities for growth rather than reasons for discouragement.

Empowering Self-Discovery and Personal Development

By committing to this self-discovery and personal development process, you are actively reshaping your relationships and reclaiming your sense of self-worth. Embrace the journey ahead with an open heart and a willingness to confront the patterns that no longer serve you, knowing that each exercise brings you closer to liberation from the chains of codependency.

Implement Activities Designed to Identify and Challenge Codependent Thoughts

The workbook provides a structured approach to recognizing and addressing codependent behaviors. Through exercises and reflections, individuals can gain clarity on their patterns of codependency. By engaging with the workbook's activities, readers can pinpoint instances of enabling unhealthy dynamics or sacrificing their well-being for others.

One exercise involves keeping a journal of interactions and emotions. By tracking these daily occurrences, individuals can start to see patterns in their behavior and feelings. This practice helps identify triggers that lead to codependent responses. Readers can challenge their automatic reactions and consider healthier alternatives through this awareness.

Another valuable activity is setting boundaries. The workbook guides individuals on establishing clear limits in their relationships, fostering a sense of self-respect and autonomy. Learning to say no when necessary is a crucial step in breaking free from codependency. By practicing assertiveness in setting boundaries, individuals can reshape their relationships based on mutual respect.

An essential aspect of challenging codependent thoughts is learning to prioritize self-care. The workbook offers exercises encouraging individuals to engage in activities that bring them joy and relaxation. By nurturing themselves, readers can develop a stronger sense of self-worth and reduce the need for external validation.

Furthermore, the workbook prompts individuals to examine their beliefs about relationships. By questioning ingrained ideas about love, sacrifice, and worthiness, readers can begin to dismantle the foundations of codependency. Challenging these deep-seated beliefs is crucial in creating new, healthier paradigms for interpersonal connections.

The workbook also includes exercises focused on identifying personal strengths and qualities. Individuals can boost their self-esteem and confidence by recognizing their inherent value and capabilities. This self-awareness forms a solid foundation for building healthier relationships based on equality and respect.

As you progress through the healing workbook, tracking your development and reflecting on your journey becomes pivotal in understanding your growth. This workbook section serves as a mirror, allowing you to observe the changes within yourself and the shifts in your relationships. Reflection is about looking back, recognizing how far you have come, and acknowledging your steps towards a healthier lifestyle.

Tracking Progress: The workbook provides structured exercises and prompts to help you monitor your progress. You can identify patterns and triggers that might lead to codependent behaviors by recording your thoughts, emotions, and reactions. This tracking mechanism enables you to see tangible evidence of your growth over time, motivating you to continue on your path to healing.

Celebrating Achievements: Take time to celebrate even the most minor victories. Acknowledge when you successfully set a boundary or practice self-care. Celebration reinforces positive behavior and encourages you to keep moving forward. Every step taken towards breaking free from codependency is a step towards reclaiming your independence and self-worth.

Reflecting on Personal Development: Regular reflection allows you to gain insight into your journey. Consider how specific exercises or activities have impacted your thoughts and feelings. Reflect on moments of clarity or instances where you found it challenging to implement new behaviors. Self-awareness is crucial in overcoming codependency, and reflecting on your experiences helps deepen that awareness.

Identifying Triggers: You can pinpoint specific triggers that lead to codependent tendencies through reflection. Whether feeling responsible for others' emotions or neglecting your needs, recognizing these triggers empowers you to respond differently in similar situations. Awareness is the first step towards change, and you can proactively address triggers by identifying triggers.

Embracing Growth Opportunities: Reflection opens doors to growth opportunities by allowing you to learn from past experiences. When reflecting on challenging situations, consider what lessons they hold for you. Every obstacle presents a chance for personal development and learning. By embracing these growth opportunities, you transform challenges into stepping stones towards a healthier mindset.

Setting Intentions: Use reflection as a tool for setting intentions for the future. Establish further growth and healing goals based on your observations and insights from tracking progress. Setting intentions helps guide your actions, providing a roadmap for continued self-improvement. Intentionality in reflection leads to purposeful steps in your journey towards breaking free from codependency.

Moving Forward: As you engage with the exercises and reflections in the workbook, remember that healing is a continuous process. Each day offers new opportunities for growth and self-discovery. By actively participating in tracking progress and reflecting on personal development, you take control of your healing journey and pave the way for lasting transformation in your relationships and sense of self-worth.

Incorporating regular reflection into your routine enhances self-awareness and reinforces the positive changes you are making in overcoming codependency. By utilizing the workbook's guidance on tracking progress and reflecting on personal development, you empower yourself to navigate challenges with newfound resilience and clarity.

The journey through understanding and overcoming codependency is both challenging and deeply rewarding. You've taken significant steps towards personal growth and emotional resilience by engaging with the practical exercises provided. The activities designed to identify and challenge codependent thoughts have equipped you with the tools to change your habitual thinking patterns, empowering you to lead a more autonomous and healthy emotional life.

Reflecting on your progress is crucial. It lets you see how far you've come and adjust your strategies. Remember, recovery is not a linear process; it involves experimentation, setbacks, and growth. Each step using this workbook is a building block in constructing a healthier, more independent self.

You are not alone in this journey. Many have walked this path and found profound transformation on the other side. Your effort and commitment to following through with these exercises demonstrate your dedication to changing your life's narrative from dependency to empowerment.

Embrace these tools with an open heart and a committed mind. The path ahead is paved with opportunities for further growth and deeper understanding. Continue to use these resources as your guide, revisiting exercises that challenge you and exploring deeper into areas where you've found significant insights.

Every day presents a new chance to reinforce your boundaries, enhance your self-awareness, and strengthen your emotional resilience. By actively participating in your recovery process, you harness the power to redefine your relationships and ultimately lead a liberated life.

Move forward with courage, knowing that each step is a progression towards recovery and renewal of your entire being.

Chapter 13: Staying the Course: Maintaining Your Newfound Freedom

"Life is a balance between holding

on and letting go."

Rumi

Embrace Your Independence: What Comes After Breaking Free?

After navigating the turbulent waters of codependency and emerging more vigorous, the real challenge begins: maintaining this newfound freedom. This stage is crucial, as it demands continuous effort and dedication to ensure that old habits do not resurface, jeopardizing progress. It's about reinforcing healthy boundaries, leveraging modern tools for independence, and committing to lifelong self-care.

The journey towards emotional autonomy is not a one-time event but an ongoing process. It involves constant vigilance in how one engages with others and oneself. Setting and maintaining boundaries might have been discussed before, but their long-term application determines success in staying liberated from codependent behaviors. It requires a clear understanding of one's limits and needs and the courage to assert them consistently in relationships.

In today's digital age, technology is pivotal in supporting individual independence. These resources are invaluable, from apps that help track mental health and wellness to online communities offering support and advice. They provide information and connectivity without dependency, allowing individuals to manage their emotional health proactively.

Furthermore, embracing a lifestyle of continuous learning is essential for personal growth and development. This pertains not only to academic knowledge but also to understanding oneself and the dynamics of relationships. Engaging in workshops, reading relevant literature, or even therapy sessions can be part of this learning process. Each step is a step towards solidifying one's sense of self and enhancing one's ability to navigate life independently.

The concept of self-care has often been misconstrued as selfishness, yet it is anything but. Prioritizing self-care means giving oneself the necessary tools and time to recharge emotionally and physically. This isn't an indulgence—it's essential maintenance for any individual who has struggled with codependency. It helps sustain the energy levels needed to enforce those crucial boundaries and supports continued personal development.

Commitment is the backbone of this entire process. Without a commitment to these practices—boundary setting, using technology for support, engaging in continuous learning, and routine self-care—the risk of reverting to old patterns remains high. Staying the course requires not just understanding these concepts but living them daily.

Thus, as we venture further into lives freed from codependency, let us remember that liberation is not merely about breaking free but staying free. It involves building a life where the dependency on others gives way to a supportive interdependence—a balance where personal well-being is prioritized and cherished.

Maintaining healthy boundaries and relationships is essential in breaking free from codependency patterns. It requires consistent effort and dedication to prioritize self-care and emotional well-being. One strategy for long-term success is regular self-reflection. Take time to assess your boundaries, feelings, and needs. Reflect on past interactions to identify areas where you may need to set firmer boundaries or communicate more effectively.

Another critical aspect of maintaining healthy relationships is communication. Be open and honest about your feelings and needs with others. Practice assertive communication, which involves expressing yourself clearly and respectfully while respecting the boundaries of others. Setting boundaries is not about controlling others but about taking care of yourself.

Self-care plays a significant role in sustaining healthy relationships. Make time for activities that nourish your mind, body, and soul. Prioritize activities that bring you joy and relaxation, whether reading a book, walking, or practicing mindfulness. Remember that self-care is not selfish; it is necessary for your well-being and the quality of your relationships.

Boundaries are crucial in maintaining healthy relationships. Establish clear boundaries with others regarding your time, energy, emotions, and physical space. Communicate these boundaries calmly but firmly, and be prepared to enforce them if crossed. Healthy boundaries protect your emotional health and prevent resentment from building up in relationships.

In addition to setting boundaries with others, it is also essential to set boundaries with yourself. This means recognizing when to say no to excessive self-criticism or perfectionism. Practice self-compassion and treat yourself with kindness and understanding. Remember that you deserve love and respect from yourself just as much as others.

To maintain healthy relationships, it is crucial to surround yourself with supportive people who respect your boundaries and encourage your personal growth. Cultivate relationships with individuals who uplift you, understand your journey towards independence, and value your well-being. Supportive relationships can provide a sense of belonging and reinforce the importance of self-care and boundary-setting.

Embracing the concept of "codependency no more" involves a commitment to prioritizing self-care, setting boundaries, fostering self-empowerment, and maintaining healthy relationships. By implementing these strategies consistently in your daily life, you can break free from unhealthy relationship patterns and cultivate a fulfilling life based on autonomy and emotional stability.

Harnessing Digital Resources for Personal Growth

In today's digital age, technology can be a powerful ally in your journey towards independence and self-empowerment. Embracing the use of various tools and resources available at your fingertips can significantly support your efforts to break free from codependent patterns and cultivate healthy relationships. Online therapy platforms offer convenient access to professional guidance and support, allowing you to work on your emotional well-being from the comfort of your own space. Mindfulness apps can assist you in developing self-awareness and managing stress, fostering a sense of inner peace and resilience.

When used mindfully, social media can connect you with like-minded individuals who share similar personal growth and empowerment goals. Joining online communities or support groups dedicated to overcoming codependency can provide a sense of belonging and encouragement. Educational websites and online courses on boundary setting, communication skills, and self-care can equip you with valuable knowledge and strategies to navigate relationships more effectively.

Journaling apps or online diaries offer a private space for reflection, helping you track your progress, identify triggers, and healthily express your thoughts and emotions. Utilize digital calendars or task management tools to schedule self-care activities, set boundaries, and prioritize your well-being. These resources can remind you of your commitment to personal growth and help you stay accountable.

When feeling overwhelmed or triggered by codependent behaviors, consider using meditation apps for relaxation and grounding exercises. Regular mindfulness can enhance your emotional regulation skills, enabling you to respond thoughtfully rather than impulsively in challenging situations. Remember that technology is a tool at your disposal; it is up to you to harness its potential for personal development and relationship growth.

By leveraging technology wisely and incorporating digital resources into your daily routine, you can reinforce your journey towards independence and self-mastery. Stay proactive in seeking tools that align with your goals of breaking free from codependency patterns and fostering healthier relationships. Empower yourself by utilizing these resources as catalysts for positive change, embracing their support in nurturing your newfound freedom from codependency.

Evaluation Framework

The Evaluation Framework is designed to assist individuals in maintaining their newfound independence and healthy relationships free from codependency. This long-term monitoring and self-assessment framework focuses on critical personal and relational health indicators. By engaging in a quarterly self-review process, readers can reflect on various aspects of their progress, rate their performance, and establish goals for improvement. The framework not only helps individuals track their development but also highlights areas that may require additional attention or support to prevent relapse into codependent patterns.

Components of the Framework

1. Maintaining Boundaries: This component focuses on establishing and upholding healthy boundaries in relationships. It involves recognizing one's needs and limits while effectively communicating them to others. Maintaining boundaries is crucial for fostering autonomy and self-respect.

2. Dependency on External Validation: This indicator evaluates how much individuals rely on external sources for validation and approval. Reducing dependency on external validation is essential for building self-confidence and self-worth from within rather than seeking constant affirmation from others.

3. Mutual Respect and Autonomy: This component assesses the presence of mutual respect, equality, and autonomy in

relationships. Healthy relationships are based on mutual support, understanding, and recognising each individual's right to independence and self-expression.

Interactions within the Framework

These components interact dynamically within the Evaluation Framework. Maintaining Boundaries lays the foundation for healthy relationships by establishing clear expectations and limits. Dependency on External Validation influences how individuals perceive themselves and their worth, affecting their ability to set boundaries effectively. Mutual Respect and Autonomy are outcomes of maintaining boundaries and reducing dependency on external validation, creating a balanced relationship dynamic.

Dynamics of the Framework

Over time, as individuals engage with the Evaluation Framework, they may experience shifts in their ability to maintain boundaries, reduce dependency on external validation, and cultivate mutual respect and autonomy in relationships. By actively participating in self-assessment and goal-setting, readers can observe progress, identify areas for growth, and make necessary adjustments to stay aligned with their recovery journey.

Practical Implications

The Evaluation Framework offers practical guidance for

individuals seeking to break free from codependency by providing a structured approach to self-assessment. By regularly evaluating their personal growth using the framework's indicators, readers can proactively address challenges, celebrate successes, and stay committed to their healing path. The framework encourages accountability, reflection, and continuous improvement in maintaining healthy boundaries and fostering empowering relationships.

In summary, the Evaluation Framework equips individuals with a systematic method for monitoring their progress in overcoming codependency. Readers can navigate their journey towards independence with clarity and purpose by focusing on critical indicators such as maintaining boundaries, reducing dependency on external validation, and cultivating mutual respect and autonomy.

Maintaining your newfound freedom from codependency is a journey of continuous growth and commitment. Developing strategies for the long-term maintenance of healthy boundaries and relationships is essential. It empowers you to navigate interpersonal dynamics effectively, ensuring you remain steadfast in your values and emotional health.

The role of technology and resources in supporting your independence cannot be overstated. Utilize these tools to foster self-sufficiency, enhance your knowledge base, and connect with supportive communities that reinforce your journey towards self-empowerment. These resources provide practical solutions that are easy to integrate into daily life, making the path to independence more accessible.

Above all, commitment to self-care and personal development is crucial. Engage actively in practices that nurture your physical, emotional, and mental well-being. Continuous learning about yourself and the dynamics of codependency will equip you with the skills to handle future challenges more effectively. This commitment enhances your quality of life and solidifies your resilience against falling back into dependent patterns.

Embrace these strategies with the understanding that each step forward is a building block towards a healthier, more autonomous future. Remember, you have the innate ability to master your emotions and overcome challenges. Taking control of your situation through these actionable steps will pave the way for a life characterized by greater fulfillment and genuine independence.

Your journey is uniquely yours, but remember that you are not alone. Each step you take is a testament to your strength and dedication to living a life free from codependency. Continue to push forward, leveraging every resource available, and always prioritize your well-being. The freedom you seek becomes a possibility and a reality through persistence and dedication.

Chapter 14: With Gratitude: Celebrating the Liberated Self

"Interdependence is the natural

order of the universe."

Dalai Lama

Embracing the Final Steps to a Truly Liberated Self

As we journey through the transformative path from codependency to self-reliance, we must pause and reflect with gratitude on our progress. Recognizing the milestones achieved fortifies our resolve and illuminates the path ahead, enriched with possibilities previously overshadowed by dependency. This critical reflection is about acknowledging change and cementing the foundation for continual growth and fulfillment.

Gratitude is a powerful tool in our arsenal against co-dependency. It allows us to see the value in each step of our journey, helping us understand that every challenge faced and every obstacle overcome has been integral to our development. By fostering a sense of thankfulness, we shift our focus from what we depended on to what we have accomplished independently, reinforcing our autonomy.

Moreover, the role of self-forgiveness in this process cannot be overstated. The journey away from codependent behaviors often unveils past decisions or actions that might bring about guilt or regret. It is vital here to employ compassion towards oneself, understanding that past actions were based on previous levels of awareness and circumstances. Learning to release this guilt is crucial in preventing it from becoming a barrier to further progress.

In dreaming big and setting long-term goals, we redefine what a fulfilling life means post-codependency. Goals are no longer framed by the needs or responses of others but are developed around our aspirations and values. This shift enhances personal satisfaction and ensures our pursuits are balanced and enriching.

Throughout "Liberated Lives," we've explored various strategies and tools designed to effectively recognize and manage codependent tendencies. From setting healthy boundaries to engaging in mindful self-care, these tactics aim to foster a robust sense of self-worth independent of others. As readers approach the culmination of this text, they are equipped not just with knowledge but with practical methods that facilitate real change in both personal and professional relationships.

The transformation chronicled here is profound—from dependency to empowerment. This evolution involves surviving without external validation and thriving through an internalized belief in one's capabilities and worth. The detailed strategies emphasized action—encouraging readers to actively apply what they've learned rather than passively consuming information.

Finally, as we wrap up our exploration into overcoming codependency within months, it's crucial to acknowledge that while the timeline may vary for each individual, the principles of commitment, awareness, and active engagement remain constant. These elements are critical in ensuring that the freedom from codependency is achieved and sustained.

Thus, as you move forward, remember that your journey might have begun with seeking freedom from codependency. Still, it blossoms into a comprehensive celebration of self-liberation—a state where your desires inform your decisions and needs rather than an obligatory response to others. Embrace this newfound independence with gratitude and confidence as you continue shaping a life of balance and fulfillment.

Reflecting on the journey from codependency to autonomy with gratitude is powerful in acknowledging personal growth and resilience. It is essential to recognize the progress made, no matter how small it may seem. Gratitude allows us to shift our focus from what we lack to what we have achieved, fostering a sense of contentment and accomplishment in our journey towards emotional freedom.

As you look back on your path of breaking free from codependent patterns, please take a moment to appreciate the courage it took to confront difficult emotions and confront ingrained behaviors. Gratitude can remind you of your strength and determination to create positive change in your life. By acknowledging the challenges you have faced and your progress, you are affirming your commitment to personal growth and self-discovery.

Expressing gratitude for the support system that has stood by you during this transformative process is also crucial. Whether it's friends, family, or a therapist, recognizing those who have offered understanding and encouragement can deepen your sense of connection and belonging. Their presence has likely been instrumental in helping you navigate the complexities of codependency and emerge stronger on the other side.

Moreover, cultivating gratitude for the lessons learned can provide valuable insights into your evolution. Every setback, every moment of doubt, and every triumph has contributed to shaping the resilient individual you are today. Embrace these experiences with an open heart, knowing each has guided you towards greater self-awareness and emotional well-being.

Incorporating gratitude into your daily practice can be a transformative tool in maintaining a positive outlook on your journey towards autonomy. Taking time each day to reflect on what you are thankful for can shift your perspective from lack to abundance, reinforcing your commitment to self-care and growth. Embrace gratitude as a beacon of light that illuminates the path ahead, reminding you of how far you have come and inspiring you to continue confidently moving forward.

Embracing Self-Forgiveness and Liberation

Self-forgiveness and releasing guilt are essential steps in the journey towards healing from codependency. It is crucial to understand that holding onto guilt and self-blame only hinders our progress and keeps us stuck in patterns of codependent behavior. By acknowledging our mistakes, learning from them, and forgiving ourselves, we can break free from the guilt and shame that often accompanies codependency. Self-forgiveness is a powerful act of self-love and compassion that allows us to release the burden of past mistakes and move forward with a sense of freedom and renewal.

Guilt is a common emotion for individuals struggling with codependency, as they often feel responsible for others' feelings and actions. However, it is vital to recognize that we are only responsible for our own emotions and behaviors, not those of others. Releasing guilt involves letting go of the belief that we are solely responsible for the well-being of others and accepting that it is okay to prioritize our own needs and boundaries. This shift in mindset can be transformative in breaking free from codependent patterns.

Practicing self-compassion is vital to the process of self-forgiveness. Instead of criticizing ourselves for past mistakes, we can offer the same kindness and understanding that we would give to a friend facing similar challenges. By treating ourselves with empathy and forgiveness, we create space for healing and growth.

It allows us to move forward with renewed self-worth and confidence.

Setting boundaries is another crucial aspect of releasing guilt in codependent relationships. By establishing clear boundaries and communicating our needs effectively, we can prevent feelings of guilt from arising when asserting our own needs or saying no to others. Boundaries are essential for maintaining healthy relationships based on mutual respect and understanding.

Journaling can be a powerful tool for processing guilt and practicing self-forgiveness. By writing about our emotions, reflecting on past experiences, and exploring our inner thoughts, we can gain clarity on guilt's root causes and release these negative emotions. Writing down affirmations or positive statements about ourselves can also help reinforce self-forgiveness.

As you embark on this journey towards a balanced and fulfilling life free from codependency, you must dream big and set long-term goals that align with your newfound sense of self. Setting goals is a powerful way to create a roadmap for your future, guiding you towards the life you envision for yourself. Begin by reflecting on what truly brings you joy, fulfillment, and a sense of purpose.

Dreaming significantly involves envisioning a life where healthy boundaries are the norm and your relationships are based on mutual respect and understanding. Picture yourself thriving in all aspects of your life, whether it's in your career, personal relationships, or self-care routines. Allow yourself to dream without limitations, embracing the possibilities of breaking free from codependent patterns.

When setting long-term goals, consider both tangible achievements and personal growth milestones. Perhaps you aspire to cultivate a strong support network of individuals who uplift and inspire you. Maybe you aim to pursue a new hobby or passion that ignites your creativity and brings you joy. Whatever your goals, ensure they resonate with the liberated self you have worked hard to nurture.

Visualize your ideal future, painting a vivid picture of what success looks like for you in a life free from codependency. Imagine confidently asserting your needs and boundaries, surrounded by relationships that nourish your soul and contribute positively to your well-being. Use this vision as motivation to take proactive steps towards making it a reality.

Break down your long-term goals into smaller, manageable steps you can work on daily. You build momentum and inch closer to your desired life by taking consistent action towards your aspirations. Celebrate every small victory along the way, acknowledging your progress towards living authentically and autonomously.

Stay committed to your vision of a fulfilling life beyond codependency, even when faced with challenges or setbacks. Remember that growth is a journey filled with ups and downs, but each obstacle presents an opportunity for learning and resilience-building. Embrace the process wholeheartedly, knowing that every step forward is a testament to your strength and determination.

In embracing your dreams for the future and setting meaningful long-term goals, you honor the transformation you have undergone in breaking free from codependency. By nurturing these aspirations, you cultivate a life grounded in self-awareness, empowerment, and authenticity—a life where your liberated self thrives unapologetically.

As we reflect on the transformative journey from codependency to autonomy, we must recognize the profound shifts that have occurred. Gratitude plays an essential role here, not just as a feeling but as a practice that reinforces your growth and newfound independence. By appreciating each step of your journey, you empower yourself to continue moving forward with confidence and resilience.

Understanding the importance of self-forgiveness is another cornerstone of liberation from codependent patterns. Letting go of guilt is not merely about alleviating emotional pain—it's about making room for growth and self-discovery. When you forgive yourself, you acknowledge your human imperfections and open up a space for learning and healing.

The encouragement to dream big and set long-term goals cannot be overstated. As you step away from codependent tendencies, envisioning a balanced, fulfilling life becomes not only possible but necessary. These dreams and goals are your roadmap to a harmonious future where your relationships and sense of self coexist.

Throughout this book, we've navigated the complexities of identifying and overcoming codependent behaviors. You've gained insights into setting healthy boundaries, fostering self-worth independent of others, and engaging in mindful self-care practices. These tools are not just strategies but parts of a new way of living that honors your individuality and enhances your relationships.

Embrace these lessons with an active mind and engaged spirit. Remember, the path to emotional wellness involves continuous effort and dedication. Each day offers a new opportunity to apply what you've learned, ensuring that every step forward makes you stronger and more connected to your true self.

You can now build healthier relationships and reclaim a life of emotional balance and personal fulfillment. Your commitment to embarking on this journey speaks volumes about your strength and capacity for change. Keep moving forward with the confidence that you can maintain lasting transformations in personal growth and relationship dynamics.

By embracing these principles, you are not just surviving; you are thriving—liberated from the chains of codependency and ready to experience all life as richness.

Epilogue

"For to be free is not merely to cast off one's chains,

but to live in a way that respects and enhances

the freedom of others."

Nelson Mandela

Embracing Your Journey Toward Self-Liberation

Reflecting on your profound journey is essential as we draw this exploration closer. You've navigated through the intricate layers of codependency, uncovering its roots and understanding how it silently orchestrates your relationships and sense of self. This is no small feat, and your courage in confronting these truths paves the way for a transformed life that celebrates your individuality and fosters genuine connections.

The practical applications of what we've discussed are vast and deeply personal. Whether in daily interactions or significant life decisions, the insights gained here can guide you to live more authentically. Implementing boundaries, practicing self-reflection, and engaging in mindful self-care are not just strategies; they are stepping stones to a liberated life.

We've revisited several vital concepts: identifying codependency traits, understanding their impact, and learning to establish healthy boundaries. Each chapter builds upon the last, creating a comprehensive framework to support your growth from awareness to action.

Consider how the principles discussed can be integrated into your routines to benefit from this book. Start small—perhaps with daily affirmations of self-worth or journaling your thoughts and feelings. These actions reinforce the mindset shifts necessary to foster independence and emotional resilience.

While this book provides many tools and insights, it is not exhaustive. The nuances of human relationships and personal psychology are vast, and there will always be more to learn. I encourage you to continue exploring these themes, perhaps by seeking out communities of others on similar paths or by engaging with a professional who can offer personalized guidance.

Taking action is crucial. You possess the innate strength needed to change your circumstances. Trust in your ability to make decisions that prioritize your well-being. As you step forward, remember that each day offers a new opportunity for growth and renewal.

Let's conclude with a thought that encapsulates our journey:

"What lies behind us and what lies before us are tiny matters compared to what lies within us."

Ralph Waldo Emerson

In these words lies a reminder of your inner strength and potential. May they inspire you as you forge a healthier, more autonomous life where your needs are recognised and celebrated. Embrace this challenge with open arms, for it is the essence of true freedom.

Conclusion

"A bird sitting on a tree is never afraid of the branch breaking,

because her trust is not on the branch but on its

own wings. Always believe in yourself."

Unknown

This exploration into personal growth and relationship dynamics marks a significant milestone in the reader's journey towards self-discovery and autonomy. The insights provided throughout the narrative serve as a mirror reflecting the intricate web of human emotions and connections and as a beacon guiding towards a brighter, more empowered future.

- Recognizing that the passage from codependency to autonomy is not linear is crucial. Each individual's experience is unique, characterized by its trials, triumphs, and moments of revelation. The path is strewn with challenges that test resilience, but these obstacles forge strength and foster deep, meaningful transformations.

- The narrative underscores the importance of self-compassion and mindfulness as indispensable companions on this voyage. By adopting a kinder, more understanding attitude towards oneself, individuals can better navigate the tumultuous waters of personal change, turning setbacks into stepping stones towards greater self-awareness and emotional intelligence.

- Another key takeaway is the redefinition of independence and interdependence. Genuine autonomy does not mean severing ties with others but instead cultivating a sense of self that is resilient in solitude and thriving in connection. It's about creating boundaries that respect personal space and invite genuine intimacy, allowing for liberating and enriching relationships.

- The role of gratitude and forgiveness in healing cannot be overstated. These practices act as the soil where the seeds of change are sown, enabling individuals to release past burdens and welcome new perspectives with an open heart. They remind us that every step of the journey, no matter how daunting, is a testament to the human spirit's capacity for growth and renewal.

- Readers need to remember that the quest for autonomy and emotional well-being is ongoing. Life will continue to present challenges, but armed with the tools and insights gained, individuals can face them with a newfound sense of confidence and clarity.

- Encouraging ongoing self-reflection and continual learning, the narrative invites readers to keep exploring the depths of their being. The ultimate goal is not to reach a final destination but to cultivate a lifestyle that celebrates growth embraces change, and honors the complexity of the human experience.

- Finally, this exploration serves as a reminder that the power to redefine one's life story, break free from the chains of codependency, and claim a path of personal liberation resides within each of us. It is a call to action for those who seek a life characterized by balance, fulfillment, and authentic connections.

Essentially, this narrative is not merely a guide but a companion on a transformative adventure towards self-realization and connection. It's a hand extended in solidarity, saying, "You are not alone on this path." The lessons it imparts are hope, courage, and the unyielding strength of the human spirit. May this journey bring light to those searching for freedom, guiding them towards a future where their potential can fully unfurl like a blossom in spring, radiant and full of promise.

Bonus Material

Your Questions, Answered!

1. How Can One Differentiate Between Healthy Dependence and Codependency in Relationships?

Differentiating between healthy dependence and codependency in relationships is a nuanced task, requiring a deep understanding of the dynamics at play. Healthy dependence is characterized by a mutual give-and-take, where both partners feel comfortable relying on each other for support, comfort, and encouragement while maintaining their identities and sense of autonomy. This dependence fosters a sense of security, trust, and strength in the relationship, allowing both individuals to grow independently and together. It is marked by clear communication, respect for boundaries, and the ability to thrive within and outside the relationship.

On the other hand, codependency emerges when one partner's need for the other becomes compulsive and demanding, leading to a relationship dynamic that is unbalanced and unhealthy. This often results from one individual's self-esteem and emotional well-being becoming overly tied to their partner's behaviors and needs, leading to blurred or non-existent personal boundaries. In a codependent relationship, there is marked difficulty in expressing one's needs or disagreements for fear of rejection or upsetting the balance, leading to an environment where genuine intimacy and growth are stifled.

Codependency also often involves a caretaking behavior where one partner enables the other's immaturity, addiction, or irresponsibility, often out of a misplaced sense of responsibility or fear of abandonment. This dynamic can prevent both individuals from addressing personal issues and patterns that need healing, perpetuating a cycle of dependency that can be challenging to break. Recognizing the signs of codependency and seeking to establish a more balanced, healthy form of dependence through open communication, setting boundaries, and fostering personal growth are crucial steps towards building stronger, healthier, and more fulfilling relationships.

2. What Are the Initial Signs of Moving From Codependency Towards Autonomy?

Moving from a state of codependency to autonomy represents a critical transition in one's personal development and relationships. This shift is often gradual and challenging to recognize, yet sure signs can indicate progress towards a more independent and self-determined life. The process involves a reevaluation of self-worth, the establishment of boundaries, and an enhanced capacity for self-reliance, marking significant milestones in the pursuit of emotional independence.

One of the initial signs is an increased sense of self-awareness. Individuals begin to understand and acknowledge their wants, needs, and emotions separate from those of others. This heightened awareness is pivotal in recognizing patterns of behavior that contribute to codependency. As individuals gain clarity about their boundaries, they will communicate them to others, asserting their needs and expectations within relationships without fear of backlash or abandonment. This step is fundamental in shifting the dynamics of existing relationships towards healthier interactions.

Another sign is the development of emotional resilience and self-sufficiency. People seek less validation and approval from others, relying more on their judgment and self-validation. This independence fosters a stronger sense of identity that is not easily swayed by others' opinions or actions. Furthermore, there's a notable improvement in handling solitude; being alone is no longer feared but embraced as an opportunity for growth and reflection. This comfort with solitude signifies a departure from the compulsive need for external companionship characteristic of codependency towards a more balanced and autonomous existence.

Additionally, moving towards autonomy involves actively working on one's self-esteem and pursuing personal interests and goals independent of others. This could manifest in taking up new hobbies, advancing in one's career, or dedicating time to individual health and wellness—endeavors that contribute to a robust sense of self and personal fulfillment. Such actions highlight a significant stride towards autonomy, illustrating an investment in one's well-being and future, detached from the approval or participation of a significant other or peer group.

In summary, the path from codependency to autonomy is marked by profound personal development, where individuals learn to prioritize their well-being, establish healthy boundaries, and cultivate a life that resonates with their values and aspirations. This transition is a testament to the human capacity for change and growth, underscored by the courage to face internal challenges and transform relational dynamics for a more balanced and fulfilling existence.

3. Can You Provide Examples of How to Set Boundaries Without Alienating Loved Ones?

Setting boundaries is crucial to establishing healthy relationships and maintaining personal well-being, yet it can often be met with resistance or misinterpretation by loved ones. Setting boundaries involves communicating your needs, limits, and expectations to others in a way that respects both your well-being and theirs. While the aim is to foster more meaningful and balanced relationships, without careful consideration, setting boundaries can sometimes be perceived as rejection or lack of care, leading to potential alienation.

To set boundaries effectively, it's essential to approach the conversation with clarity, empathy, and assertiveness. Start by clearly identifying your needs and the boundaries that must be in place to respect those needs. This step requires self-reflection and honesty about what behaviors you find acceptable and what limits are necessary for your mental and emotional health. When communicating these boundaries to loved ones, use "I" statements to express how certain behaviors affect you personally rather than placing blame or making accusatory remarks. For example, saying, "I feel overwhelmed when we spend every weekend together, and I need some time to recharge," centers the conversation on your needs and feelings without implying fault on the other person's part.

In addition to clear communication, it's essential to be consistent and compassionate in enforcing your boundaries. Consistency reinforces your commitment to your well-being and helps others understand the seriousness of your requests. Meanwhile, approaching the conversation with empathy, acknowledging how your boundaries might affect your loved ones, and being open to their feelings and responses can help prevent feelings of alienation. Recognize that initial reactions might be mixed, but as boundaries become a regular part of the relationship over time, they can lead to more profound mutual respect and understanding.

Furthermore, offering alternatives or compromises when appropriate can help mitigate feelings of rejection or alienation. For example, if you need time to yourself, suggest times when you will be fully present and available to spend quality time together. This approach demonstrates that setting boundaries isn't about pushing loved ones away but ensuring that the time you spend together is healthy, balanced, and enriching for all involved.

In sum, setting boundaries without alienating loved ones involves clear, empathetic communication, consistency in maintaining your boundaries, and, where possible, offering solutions that acknowledge the needs and feelings of both parties. This careful balance allows for personal growth and healthier relationships, fostering an environment where individuality and togetherness can thrive.

4. In What Ways Does Mindfulness Specifically Contribute to Overcoming Codependency?

Mindfulness, the practice of being fully present and engaged in the moment without judgment, is pivotal in overcoming codependency by promoting self-awareness and emotional regulation. Individuals with codependent tendencies often find themselves entangled in the emotional states and needs of others, sometimes at the expense of their well-being and identity. Through mindfulness, one learns to observe one's thoughts, feelings, and reactions without immediately acting upon them, creating a space of awareness that can help differentiate between one's emotions and those of others. This increased self-awareness is crucial for recognizing and addressing codependent behaviors, as it allows individuals to identify moments when they are sacrificing their own needs or overstepping boundaries to care for or please someone else.

Furthermore, mindfulness teaches individuals to confront and sit with uncomfortable emotions, such as loneliness, anxiety, or rejection, without seeking external validation or companionship to mitigate these feelings. This aspect of emotional regulation is significant for overcoming codependency, which is often characterized by a fear of abandonment and an excessive reliance on others for a sense of security and self-worth. Mindfulness practices such as meditation, mindful breathing, or body scans can help individuals learn to soothe themselves and manage distressing emotions independently, lessening the compulsive need for external validation.

By cultivating mindfulness, individuals working to overcome codependency can also develop greater compassion towards themselves, recognizing that self-care and setting boundaries are acts of self-respect rather than selfishness. This self-compassion encourages a healthier approach to interpersonal relationships, where one can express love and care for others without losing sight of their needs and well-being. Ultimately, mindfulness enables a transformation from codependent patterns towards healthier, more autonomous ways of relating to oneself and others, grounded in a deep sense of inner stability and self-reliance.

In essence, mindfulness contributes to overcoming codependency by fostering self-awareness, regulating emotions, and promoting self-compassion. These benefits collectively support individuals in establishing healthier relationships and a more balanced sense of self, characteristics that are often undermined by codependent dynamics. Through regular mindfulness practice, individuals learn to prioritize their well-being, set appropriate boundaries, and develop a fulfilling life that does not depend on the approval or presence of others.

5. Are There Particular Life Events That Typically Trigger the Shift From Codependency to Autonomy?

Several life events can serve as pivotal points, prompting individuals to transition from patterns of codependency to autonomy. These events often carry significant emotional weight or result in profound changes in one's life circumstances, creating an environment ripe for introspection and change. Examples of such life events include the end of a relationship, significant health diagnoses, the loss of a loved one, experiences of trauma, or even the process of aging. Each of these situations can catalyze a profound reevaluation of one's life and relationships, uncovering codependent tendencies that might have been previously overlooked or normalized.

The end of a significant relationship, be it romantic, familial, or a close friendship, often exposes the extent of one's reliance on others for emotional support, decision-making, and self-worth. This realization can be incredibly jarring, leading an individual to confront their fears of abandonment and loneliness directly. Such confrontation, although painful, creates an opportunity for growth. It invites the individual to develop new coping strategies, foster a stronger sense of self, and explore personal needs and desires that were previously sidelined. This process of self-discovery and the subsequent adoption of healthier relational patterns mark the beginning of the shift towards autonomy.

Similarly, facing a significant health diagnosis or the loss of a loved one can starkly highlight the impermanence of life and the importance of self-reliance. The emotional turmoil associated with these events may initially intensify codependent behaviors as a coping mechanism. However, as the individual begins to process their grief and adapt to new realities, a significant shift in perspective often occurs. This shift typically involves a greater appreciation for personal health, well-being, and the necessity of setting boundaries that protect one's mental and emotional space. The resultant growth fosters a sense of autonomy, enabling individuals to engage in reciprocal and nurturing relationships rather than ones marked by dependency and sacrifice.

In essence, such life events thrust individuals into scenarios that starkly contrast their usual modes of operation, compelling them to face and reevaluate deep-seated fears and behaviors. Through these challenging times, the seeds of autonomy are sown. Individuals learn the importance of caring for themselves, vocalizing their needs, and crafting a life that reflects their true desires and values. This transformation is not instantaneous but rather a gradual process of adopting new ways of thinking and relating to oneself and others. A profound internal shift marks the move from codependency to autonomy, often catalyzed by life's turning points and leads to a more balanced and fulfilled existence.

6. How Does the Process of Self-Forgiveness Differ From Ordinary Forgiveness in the Context of Codependency?

Self-forgiveness in codependency involves a more profound, personal process than ordinary forgiveness. This distinction arises from the need to confront and accept one's part in developing and perpetuating codependent behaviors, which often stem from long-standing patterns of thinking and behavior. Unlike ordinary forgiveness, which typically extends to others for their actions or offenses, self-forgiveness requires individuals to grapple with their own mistakes, misjudgments, and the subsequent impact on their lives and relationships. This reflective process is critical in overcoming codependency, as it encourages individuals to acknowledge their vulnerabilities and how they might have neglected their needs or compromised their values in the pursuit of external validation or affection.

The process of self-forgiveness in overcoming codependency begins with the recognition of one's worth independently of others' approval. It involves acknowledging the harm that codependent behaviors have caused both to oneself and to others, and it requires taking responsibility for one's role in these dynamics without lapsing into self-blame. This is a delicate balance, where the aim is to cultivate compassion towards oneself, recognizing that codependent patterns often originate as survival strategies in response to past trauma or unmet emotional needs.

Self-forgiveness becomes a vehicle for healing, allowing individuals to release guilt and shame associated with their past actions or choices, thereby facilitating a shift towards healthier ways of relating to oneself and others.

Furthermore, self-forgiveness in the context of codependency paves the way for genuine change. It involves acknowledging past actions and attitudes and actively working to develop new, healthier patterns of behavior. This might include setting boundaries, prioritizing self-care, and learning to seek fulfillment internally rather than through external relationships or validation. Unlike ordinary forgiveness, which is an act extended to another, self-forgiveness is an ongoing process of self-evaluation and adjustment. It requires patience, effort, and a commitment to personal growth. Through self-forgiveness, individuals can loosen the grip of codependency, gradually moving towards a state of autonomy where their self-worth is not contingent on the perceptions or actions of others. This profound transformation reflects a deep reconciliation with oneself that is foundational for establishing balanced, healthy relationships moving forward.

7. Could You Explore the Role of Childhood Experiences in Forming Codependent Behaviors?

Childhood experiences play a pivotal role in the development of codependent behaviors, often laying the foundation for these patterns to emerge in adult relationships. From a young age, individuals learn to interpret and respond to their environment, with family dynamics significantly influencing their understanding of self-worth, love, and how they relate to others. In families where emotional expressiveness is stifled, where there is a high degree of dysfunction, or where the child's needs are consistently overlooked in favor of a caregiver's demands, the seeds of codependency are sown. Children in these environments may learn to prioritize the well-being and needs of others above their own, equating love and acceptance with self-sacrifice and suppressing their own needs and feelings.

This early conditioning can lead individuals to develop a distorted sense of self, where their identity and self-worth become excessively tied to their ability to care for, please, or meet the needs of others. Such dynamics are particularly prevalent in households affected by substance abuse, mental illness, or chronic illness, where a child might take on caregiver roles prematurely, often referred to as "parentification". This role shifts not only burdens the child with adult responsibilities but also reinforces the belief that their value is contingent upon their utility or ability to solve problems for others, setting the stage for future codependent relationships.

The transition from childhood into adulthood does not automatically rectify these learned behaviors. Instead, without conscious effort and intervention, these patterns tend to persist, influencing selections in relationships and the dynamics within them. Adults with codependent tendencies often find themselves in relationships where they feel a compulsion to fix, save, or change their partner, reflecting their childhood attempts to mend or stabilize their family environment. Recognizing and addressing the roots of codependency in one's childhood is crucial for healing. It involves unpacking the complex layers of past experiences, acknowledging their impact, and working towards establishing healthier relational patterns. This deep, introspective work is essential for breaking the cycle of codependency, paving the way for relationships grounded in mutual respect, autonomy, and genuine connection.

8. What Strategies Can Be Employed to Maintain Emotional Balance While Navigating the Path to Autonomy?

Maintaining emotional balance is crucial when navigating the path to autonomy, particularly for individuals overcoming codependency. This process entails a conscientious effort towards self-awareness and managing one's emotional landscape. A fundamental strategy involves the cultivation of mindfulness and presence. By actively engaging in mindfulness practices, individuals can develop heightened awareness of their thoughts, feelings, and bodily sensations without judgment. This presence of mind enables one to recognize and assess their emotional responses to various stimuli or interactions, distinguishing between reactions stemming from past conditioning and those aligned with their current values and goals. Mindfulness thus serves as a tool for individuals to remain centered and balanced, even when confronted with emotional triggers that might previously have led to codependent behaviors.

Additionally, developing a robust support system is indispensable in maintaining emotional balance. This network may include friends, family members who understand and support the individual's quest for autonomy, therapists, and peer support groups. Such a support system provides a sounding board for sharing experiences and challenges and a source of feedback, encouragement, and perspective. Engaging with others on similar journeys or who have navigated their paths to autonomy can be particularly validating and enlightening. It underscores the importance of not isolating oneself during this transitional phase, reminding individuals that seeking help and connection is not indicative of weakness but rather a courageous step towards self-reliance and emotional resilience.

Finally, establishing and adhering to boundaries is pivotal in maintaining emotional equilibrium. This involves identifying and communicating one's needs, limits, and expectations in relationships and other areas of life. Setting boundaries is an exercise in self-respect and respect for others, delineating the space for personal growth and cultivating healthy, balanced relationships. It requires assertiveness and the willingness to stand firm even when faced with resistance or criticism. Through boundary-setting, individuals learn to prioritize their well-being and respect their own needs, facilitating a nurturing environment for the development of autonomy. Fluid and regular reflection on these boundaries ensure they remain relevant and supportive of the individual's evolving independence and emotional health. Together, mindfulness, a supportive community, and clear boundaries constitute a triad of strategies essential for sustaining emotional balance from codependency to autonomy.

9. How Do You Suggest Dealing With Setbacks or Relapses Into Codependent Patterns?

Dealing with setbacks or relapses into codependent behaviors is an inevitable part of the recovery and growth process; recognizing this fact is the first step towards managing them effectively. These moments do not signify failure but are important indicators of underlying issues that may still need attention and resolution. The key to addressing these setbacks is fostering a compassionate and non-judgmental attitude towards oneself. It's crucial to understand that recovery from deeply ingrained codependent patterns is a gradual and often non-linear process. Instead of viewing relapses as regressions, they can be seen as opportunities for learning and deeper self-reflection. This perspective encourages individuals to analyze the triggers or circumstances that led to the fallback, enhancing their understanding of their emotional vulnerabilities and resilience mechanisms.

Upon recognizing a setback, engaging in constructive self-dialogue and seeking support where necessary is vital. This can involve revisiting therapeutic practices, talking to a trusted friend or mentor, or participating in support groups where individuals can share their experiences and strategies for overcoming similar challenges. These actions provide immediate relief and a sense of belonging and reinforce the person's commitment to their recovery path. Additionally, revisiting and possibly revising individual goals and strategies for achieving autonomy and emotional balance can be beneficial. Reflecting on whether current practices align with personal aspirations and making adjustments as needed ensures that one's approach to recovery remains dynamic and responsive to one's evolving needs.

Finally, strengthening one's coping mechanisms and preventive strategies plays a crucial role in mitigating the impact of future setbacks. This could mean enhancing mindfulness practices, identifying and planning for potential triggers, and improving communication skills for better boundary setting. Regularly practicing these skills in varied situations builds confidence and competence in handling emotional challenges without resorting to codependent behaviors. Furthermore, committing to a lifestyle that supports overall well-being, including physical health, social connections, and personal interests, creates a solid foundation for enduring autonomy and emotional stability. Understanding the nature of setbacks, extending kindness to oneself during these times, actively seeking support, and refining recovery strategies contribute significantly to navigating and overcoming the challenges of breaking free from codependent patterns.

10. Is There a Way to Measure Progress in the Transition From Codependency to Autonomy?

Measuring progress in the transition from codependency to autonomy can be complex due to the personal and subjective nature of these concepts. However, several qualitative and quantitative ways exist to assess growth and development in this area. Understanding that this transition is a deeply personal process, progress measurement largely relies on individual reflection and self-assessment, complemented by feedback from trusted support networks.

One practical approach to evaluating progress is through self-reflection and journaling. Individuals can set specific, measurable goals related to autonomy and emotional independence. These goals can include developing and maintaining boundaries, increasing time spent on personal interests, and reducing the frequency of codependent relationship behaviors. Regular journal entries can help track these changes over time, providing a written record of successes, challenges, and insights gained along the way. This process helps recognise progress and identify areas that may require further attention or different strategies.

Additionally, feedback from therapists, close friends, or support groups can offer a valuable external perspective on an individual's development. These sources can provide objective observations on behavior, communication, and emotional resilience changes, which might not be fully apparent to the individual. Furthermore, therapy or counseling can provide professional assessment and guidance on the progress towards autonomy. Therapists can use various tools and techniques to help individuals evaluate their growth, including standardized assessments that measure emotional independence, self-esteem, and relationship dynamics.

Beyond self-assessment and external feedback, progress can also be observed in enhancing daily functioning and overall well-being. Signs such as decreased anxiety in decision-making, more assertive communication, and improved conflict-resolution skills can indicate growth towards autonomy. Participation in new activities, expansion of social networks, and a willingness to explore personal interests without fear of judgment or reliance on others further underscore this advancement.

In conclusion, while there's no one-size-fits-all metric for measuring progress in the transition from codependency to autonomy, self-reflection, goal-setting, journaling, and seeking feedback from supportive relationships and professionals can offer comprehensive insights. Observing changes in one's thoughts, behaviors, and emotional responses over time provides a nuanced understanding of personal growth, guiding ongoing efforts towards achieving greater autonomy and emotional health.

11. How Can One Cultivate Gratitude in Challenging Times, Especially When Struggling With Codependency Issues?

Cultivating gratitude during challenging times, particularly amidst the struggles with codependency, can seem like a formidable task. Yet, during these moments, gratitude can serve as a potent tool for emotional resilience and a shift in perspective. Gratitude encourages individuals to acknowledge the positive aspects of their lives, even when overshadowed by difficulties, thereby fostering a sense of well-being and reducing the impact of distressing emotions and situations.

One approach to cultivating gratitude involves the practice of daily reflection on things one is thankful for. This can be as simple as acknowledging a person's kindness, the beauty of nature, personal achievement, or home comfort. Integrating this practice into one's routine can significantly shift focus from codependency-related issues and challenges towards appreciation of the present. A gratitude journal accelerates this process by offering a tangible record of positive experiences and thoughts, reinforcing their impact over time.

Furthermore, practicing mindfulness and meditation can enhance one's capacity for gratitude. Mindfulness encourages living in the moment and recognizing the value of current experiences rather than being preoccupied with past regrets or future worries related to codependent patterns. Meditation, specifically gratitude meditation, further enables individuals to focus on appreciating the positive aspects of their lives, facilitating a deeper connection to themselves and reducing the compulsive need for external validation or control.

Engaging in acts of kindness and expressing gratitude to others can also amplify feelings of appreciation. In the context of overcoming codependency, such actions can shift the focus from seeking validation or support from others to acknowledging the interconnectedness of human experiences and the joy of giving without expectations. This fosters a healthier relationship balance and enhances self-esteem by recognising one's agency and the positive impact one can have on others' lives.

In conclusion, cultivating gratitude amidst the challenges of dealing with codependency issues can play a crucial role in the recovery process. It offers a constructive way to reinterpret personal narratives, focusing on growth, resilience, and life's simple yet profound aspects that bring joy and fulfillment. By integrating gratitude practices into daily life, individuals can make significant strides toward emotional autonomy and well-being, gradually decreasing the influence of codependent behaviors and thought patterns.

## 12.	What Role Does Self-Compassion Play in the Healing Process, and How Can It Be Developed?

Self-compassion is a critical component of the healing process, especially for individuals grappling with the aftermath of codependency. It entails treating oneself with the same kindness, concern, and support one would offer a good friend facing similar issues. This approach to self-care and understanding fosters a nurturing inner environment that promotes emotional healing and resilience. By adopting a stance of self-compassion, individuals learn to acknowledge their suffering without judgment, recognize their common humanity, and maintain a balanced awareness of their emotions.

Developing self-compassion can be challenging, particularly for those accustomed to self-criticism or who have internalized negative beliefs about themselves as a result of codependent relationships. However, there are practical strategies that can facilitate this growth. One method is mindfulness meditation, which encourages individuals to observe their thoughts and feelings with openness and curiosity rather than judgment. Such practices help recognise and accept one's emotional state without being overwhelmed. Additionally, exercises that specifically focus on cultivating compassion towards oneself, such as writing letters to oneself from a compassionate perspective, can significantly enhance self-compassion.

Another essential aspect of developing self-compassion involves challenging and changing the internalized negative narratives that fuel feelings of unworthiness and shame. This can be achieved through cognitive-behavioral techniques that identify and question these harmful beliefs, replacing them with more compassionate and constructive thoughts. Engaging in therapy or support groups where experiences are shared in a non-judgmental environment can also reinforce the understanding that suffering and imperfection are part of the shared human experience, thereby reducing feelings of isolation and self-criticism. Furthermore, setting realistic goals for personal growth and acknowledging even small progress can boost self-confidence and reinforce a compassionate self-view.

In conclusion, self-compassion is indispensable in healing from codependency by allowing individuals to relate to themselves in a kinder, more understanding manner. It is a foundation for emotional resilience, enabling people to navigate their healing process with more tremendous patience and less self-judgment. Developing self-compassion requires intention and practice but can lead to profound changes in how one relates to oneself and navigates challenges. Individuals can significantly enhance their self-compassion through mindfulness, cognitive restructuring, and cultivating a supportive community, facilitating a healthier and more autonomous emotional life.

13.   Are There Specific Exercises or Practices Recommended for Strengthening One's Sense of Autonomy?

Strengthening one's sense of autonomy is crucial in overcoming codependency and fostering a healthy, self-directed life. Autonomy involves having a sense of self-determination, where an individual feels capable of making their own choices and can act according to their values and interests rather than continually seeking approval or direction from others. For those who have struggled with codependent relationships, developing a stronger sense of autonomy can be both challenging and liberating.

One effective exercise for enhancing autonomy is the establishment of personal boundaries. This practice involves clearly defining what is acceptable and what is not in terms of treatment by others and understanding one's own limits and needs. Setting and maintaining healthy boundaries requires self-awareness and the confidence to assert one's rights and needs, which are essential components of autonomy. Regular reflection through journaling about experiences related to these boundaries can provide insights into how well one maintains one's sense of self in various relationships and situations.

Another practice is decision-making exercises, which encourage individuals to choose based on their preferences rather than external expectations. This can start with small decisions, such as choosing a meal based on personal preference rather than what they think others would approve of, and gradually progress to more significant life choices, such as career moves or relationship decisions. Making a habit of evaluating decisions based on one's values and desires reinforces an internal locus of control, which is pivotal for autonomy.

Engaging in activities that promote self-discovery and self-reliance also strengthens autonomy. This could include solo hobbies, learning new skills, or undertaking challenges that require personal initiative and problem-solving. Such activities allow individuals to explore their interests and capabilities away from the influence of others, contributing to a stronger sense of self and independence.

In conclusion, developing a stronger sense of autonomy involves a multi-faceted approach that includes setting personal boundaries, practicing independent decision-making, and engaging in self-discovery activities. These practices help individuals reduce their dependency on others for approval and direction and foster a deeper understanding of their own values, needs, and capabilities. This process of building autonomy is integral to the healing journey from codependency, leading towards a more empowered and self-determined life.

14. How Does Redefining Independence and Interdependence Affect Personal and Professional Relationships?

Redefining independence and interdependence is crucial in shaping personal and professional relationships by fostering healthier dynamics, promoting mutual respect, and enhancing communication. In this context, independence refers to an individual's ability to maintain their sense of self-identity, make decisions, and pursue their interests without relying on others' approval or support. On the other hand, Interdependence acknowledges the value of supportive and collaborative relationships where parties influence each other positively while maintaining their autonomy.

In personal relationships, this redefinition encourages individuals to pursue their passions and interests independently, contributing to a more robust sense of self and personal fulfillment. It allows people to enter relationships not out of neediness or a fear of being alone but from a desire to share their lives with someone in a balanced and healthy way. This balance reduces the strain typically placed on relationships by codependency, where one or both parties depend heavily on the other for their emotional well-being or identity. By fostering independence, individuals can come together in a space of mutual respect and personal integrity, where their love and support for each other are not conditions for their self-worth but expressions of their shared values and respect.

In the professional realm, redefining independence and interdependence can lead to a more innovative, engaging, and productive work environment. Employees who feel autonomous are more likely to take initiative, contribute original ideas, and pursue excellence in their tasks because they see the value in their work beyond external validation. At the same time, an interdependent work culture values collaboration, acknowledging that the combined strengths and contributions of the team are greater than the sum of its parts. This approach can lead to more effective problem-solving, improved communication, and a stronger sense of community among colleagues, critical factors in organizational success.

Furthermore, redefining these concepts can greatly improve conflict resolution and resilience in both personal and professional settings. By respecting autonomy, individuals are more likely to approach disagreements with the understanding that different perspectives can coexist and contribute to a more comprehensive understanding of issues. Meanwhile, a sense of healthy interdependence ensures that conflicts are navigated with the awareness that the relationship's integrity is more important than winning an argument, fostering a culture of constructive feedback and mutual growth.

Overall, redefining independence and interdependence within relationships marks a shift towards more fulfilling and respectful connections. It emphasizes the importance of personal growth and responsibility while recognizing the fundamental human need for connection and support. This balanced approach enhances individual well-being and strengthens the fabric of interpersonal and professional relationships, leading to more harmonious and effective collaborations.

15. In What Ways Can One Encourage a Partner or Loved One to Support Their Journey From Codependency to Autonomy Without Imposing on Their Freedom or Autonomy?

Encouraging a partner or loved one to support one's transition from codependency to autonomy is a delicate process that requires clear communication, understanding, and mutual respect. It begins with an open dialogue where the individual seeking autonomy explains their needs, reasons, and how their partner can support them. This conversation should emphasize that seeking autonomy is not a rejection of the partner or their importance in the individual's life but a step towards a healthier, more balanced relationship. It's crucial to make it understood that autonomy enhances personal growth, which in turn can deepen and enrich the relationship.

Setting boundaries is an essential component of this process. Encouraging a partner to support one's autonomy involves establishing clear boundaries around time, space, and activities. These boundaries allow individuals seeking autonomy to explore their interests, make decisions independently, and develop a sense of self outside the relationship. It is essential to reassure the partner that setting boundaries is not about creating distance but a healthy space for individual growth that benefits both parties. Regular check-ins can help both partners to adjust and respect these boundaries over time, ensuring that they are maintained in a way that supports the relationship.

Additionally, this process involves encouraging the partner to pursue their interests and develop their sense of autonomy. This mutual growth fosters a deeper understanding and appreciation for each other's need for independence and interdependence. It can help prevent feelings of neglect or abandonment, as both individuals are engaged in a common goal of self-improvement and balance. The couple can transform their relationship into a more dynamic, resilient, and fulfilling partnership by supporting each other in this journey.

Moving from codependency to autonomy in a partnership fosters an environment where both individuals feel free to be themselves while still being part of a committed relationship. It's about finding a balance where personal growth and relational intimacy coexist and enhance each other. By approaching this transition with openness, patience, and commitment, partners can create a stronger, more balanced connection that allows both individuals to thrive.

Thank You

We sincerely hope that this exploration into the dynamic dance of independence and interdependence has provided you with valuable insights for nurturing healthier, more fulfilling relationships in every area of your life.

Thank you for allowing us to share our perspectives and strategies with you. It's our greatest wish that the ideas presented here inspire you to take meaningful steps towards personal growth and deeper connections with those around you.

May your journey from codependency to autonomy be enriching, empowering, and rewarding.